PATHWAY
THROUGH LOSS

Pathway Through Loss

Finding Hope in the Dark Valleys

Bertha Brannen

ISBN: Hardcover   978-1-7960-3166-9
               Softcover   978-1-7960-3165-2
               eBook   978-1-7960-3164-5

Print information available on the last page.

Rev. date: 05/03/2019

To order additional copies of this book, contact:
Xlibris
1-888-795-4274
www.Xlibris.com
Orders@Xlibris.com
791088

CONTENTS

If Alice had not been born, lived, and died, this book would never have been written.

ALICE RUBY

Alice Ruby, as she liked to introduce herself, was born the sixth child of a family of nine in the early 1950s in what would be considered an impoverished village by today's standard. The scarcity of home comforts was cushioned by strong family ties and a good dose of humor. Alice ran with the humor. By age twenty-five, she had graduated from a nursing program in Halifax, returned home, and secured full-time employment at the local hospital. She married her handsome high school sweetheart, who had built their new home, and their "happily ever after" life began. The spark in their relationship was sometimes illuminated by Alice's determination to flirt. A vivid recollection of mine is her husband leaving her standing on the dance floor as she was pretending to have a toothache in order to gain the attention of the good-looking dentist dancing nearby. My memory files hold stories upon stories embraced by peals of laughter brought on by her antics. Her husband was not surprised how when their first child's head was crowning, Alice, between contractions, said to the young family doctor, "At last we meet face-to-face." She had spunk. She was in love. She was happy. She would tell people that Elvis was her real dad, proven not by DNA but by the obvious fact that she was the only sibling with jet-black hair.

Before her son turned two, Alice was admitted to the local hospital with a diagnosis of pneumonia. I clearly recall the medical internist calling me away from my nursing duties, asking to speak to me in the hospital stairwell. He explained that he was fairly certain that Alice had Goodpasture's syndrome, a rare autoimmune disease in which one's antibodies destroy the membranes in both the lungs and kidneys. As a registered nurse having practiced for several years, I had never heard of the disease. Her diagnosis was confirmed two weeks later after she was transferred to the larger city hospital.

Alice spent many weeks in hospital for dialysis treatment, followed by respiratory and renal (kidney) complications. Following bilateral nephrectomy (surgical removal of kidneys), a procedure intended to slow the attack of her antibodies and hopefully prolong her life, she shared with a visiting aunt that she had her kidneys removed as toilet tissue was getting too expensive.

Alice's journey was a difficult one, and it affected everyone who loved her. Her young husband was by her side whenever he was not at work. In typical fashion, loss was expressed, or not, in as many different ways as there are individual personalities. Some expressed loss right away, while others tended to avoid the issue depending on learned behaviors, societal expectations, or both. Although many family members and friends were open to talking about the challenges that Alice faced, not everyone was prepared to share their own emotional roller coaster.

With a full and happy life ahead at age twenty-six, a terminal illness was the last thing Alice expected. Facing her death was difficult enough. However, she would suffer multiple losses on the journey ahead, but she rarely complained.

Loss of self-esteem often accompanies negative changes in body image. Most of us have fretted over a bad hair day or tried desperately to conceal a cold sore before presenting ourselves to the public. We have all heard apologies from persons we meet, excusing their appearance for reasons not so obvious to us. My deceased spouse, George, was left with a significant limp and limited use of his right arm following his stroke. He would often avoid public places, jokingly saying, "Nobody wants to see a cripple."

Alice commented on her appearance as her disease quickly changed, and she became disfigured by puffiness, pale skin, weight gain, and an exaggerated forward curvature of her neck and upper spine. She would stretch up out of her chair, lean closer to the mirror over her hospital bathroom sink, stick her tongue out, and ask the stranger looking back at her, "Chi s'que t'est toi? Et eyou s'tu d'vonne?" (Who are you, and where did you come from?) Her courage often broke my heart.

Alice lost all her ability to care for her young son. The home she dreamt about was too often being viewed from her bed. The loss of a dream for herself, for her husband, and for her family became her reality. She spent a lot of time in the local hospital for long hours of dialysis and weeks in the larger city hospital, a four-hour drive from home, away from the familiarity, comfort, and love of family.

Privacy is next to impossible to maintain when under the care of a health-care team. Alice required insertion of a needle in her groin. As common practice in the 1970s, hair removal was routine in the prepping of a sterile site. Alice asked the nurse if he could leave her with a heart-shaped design as it would be a nice surprise for her husband. Her humor always made the staff feel at ease. She trudged on in as positive a manner as I had ever witnessed in my forty-seven years of nursing.

Our mother had died from cancer in 1969. Mom entered the hospital for a hysterectomy in January and died six months later. During her short illness and deteriorating health, we continued to reassure her that she would get better. Alice knew we had ignored our mother's questions about her illness, as it was a common medical and nursing practice in those years. I have a clear recollection of mom's surgeon telling me of her devastating diagnosis, adding, "We won't tell your father [or your mother]."

When Alice's illness progressed, she asked me if she was going to die. Before I could answer, she said, "Don't lie to me!" And I did not lie as we had lied to my mom.

Growing up, Alice and I shared a bed and the secrets of childhood. With only fifteen-month difference in age, we had similar interests, plus she was easy to get along with. Our closeness and shared profession set the stage for honesty. It was through her palliative journey that Alice became my teacher. She knew she could not be cured. She needed to talk and to plan, and I needed to listen. By accepting the openness of her conversations, I was privileged to hear her innermost thoughts on leaving this earth and, most important to her, choosing the person who would help her husband in the care of her two-year-old son. A mother must have that opportunity. She chose the person whom she knew would be an excellent caregiver.

The 1970s brought new religions to our predominately Roman Catholic community, and some born-again Christians, as they called themselves, decided they should visit Alice in the hospital and save her soul by converting her to their belief. She told them to get out! These well-intended individuals were also visiting healthy members of the community, eagerly doing house calls. They knocked on my brother's door. He invited them in, listened to their conversion theory, and asked if they could indeed save the most awful sinners.

"Even women of ill repute?" he asked.

"Yes, of course we can!"

"Great! Save me one for Saturday night!"

I assume those well-intended visitors did restore the faith of some, but they did not return to visit any of my siblings.

Alice died in the spring of 1977 while the village was occupied with kiack fishing season. On the day prior to her death, she was radiant as she shared a vivid dream where she was walking along the most beautiful path and felt the presence of the Virgin Mary. "I will walk again!" she said to me.

It was years later that I came across an old school scribble of Alice's that I did not recall was in my possession. I read these words that she had written in 1965: "Notre Seigneur a fait les roses, les oiseaux et la belle nature, mais la plus belle chose q'il a fait, c'est Le cœur d'une maman." (Our Savior created the roses, the birds, and the beauty of nature, but the most beautiful thing he created is the heart of a mother.) Her faith was grounded in what she had been taught and believed until her death.

Her son had turned two in February. He told everyone he came in contact with that his Mame, as he called her, has gone to the kayak brook. Many months later, when his dad had to take him to the ER in the local hospital, that young boy made a huge fuss. He wanted to go upstairs to see his Mame.

Following Alice's death in 1977, I embarked on a journey that focused on listening to my patients facing critical illness. I read numerous articles on dying and death and pursued and attended numerous seminars and university courses connected to the topic.

In 1999, when my young husband died, I knew that I had information that would ease my journey. I thought I knew. I was wrong. I was overwhelmed by the support I received that first week after his death. I was equally frustrated by the silence from family and friends once his burial was over. I felt as though everyone had forgotten that he ever lived. Nobody spoke his name. I wanted to hear his name. After George's death, I would wake up each day reliving his illness while missing that huge part of my life. I pictured his cold body lying lifeless where I had found him upon returning from church on that cold December day. It bothered me even more, thinking that he was naked, lying on that cold floor. He had walked in the kitchen from the shower, towel in hand, where he took his last step and his last breath. I shared my feelings with my youngest son, and he said, "Mom, it's fitting that we enter the world naked, and he left the world naked." At that time, those were the words that I needed to hear. That vision of him on the floor took on a new meaning for me. George had completed his journey on earth.

Weeks later, I was driving George's truck and indulging in self-pity, focusing on all that had been lost. For no obvious reason, the sun visor fell open, and his pen fell onto my lap. It made me forget my anger. It made me laugh, probably for the first time since his death. I forgot about feeling sorry for myself. It was as if he was saying, "Smarten up. The rest of your life is yet to be lived!"

As I was getting ready for work one morning, I entered the bathroom to the strong scent of his aftershave. Thinking some liquid must have spilled under the sink vanity, I found myself on my hands and knees emptying everything in that space. As I looked at the contents spread on the floor and realized there never was a spill, I sat dumbfounded. Was he sending me a sign? Was I losing my mind? I chose the latter explanation and therefore did not share this experience with anyone, except in group years later. Many had stories of unexplainable events following the death of their loved one. Maybe we were not crazy after all.

I was referred to a neurologist and had brain scans and other medical investigations following recurring visions bordering on hallucinations. I would first experience a warm sensation over my entire body prior to feeling as though I was entering a dreamlike state. I heard voices clearly talking in hushed and cheerful voices behind what appeared to be a thin see-through curtain. I could see each detail of their environment, including the windows dressed in pretty patterned curtains. I always saw men, and one in particular resembled Andy Gibb of the band the Bee Gees. Although I liked that band, it did not hold any significance for me. If I was interrupted in any way while in these visions, I would find it extremely difficult to focus on the present moment. I hid these sensations on numerous occasions as they were difficult to explain, and part of my thinking was that I was just feeling too weird to talk about it. At the same time, I was so drawn to the feelings I experienced that I wanted more. These sensations continued at random times and places for a couple of years following George's death, and then they stopped. All medical investigations proved negative. One possible explanation was offered: a dumping of chemicals and hormones in my system as a result of grief may have created intermittent feelings of euphoria associated with hallucinations.

I contemplated that other grievers must have felt some of the confusion I was feeling. I decided to form a community support group. Months after being widowed, I purchased a DVD program on grief. The educational videos and workbook exercises provided participants with an opportunity to learn about their grief journey and to share it with others. I did not realize at the time that the group would help me as much as I would help them.

Healing requires acknowledgment of the emotions. Healing requires time spent being listened to and having emotions validated. My definition of healing is getting to that place where you remember the person for what they gave you in life rather than what they took away by dying.

Twenty years later, I now facilitate my own program based on new material and participant evaluations. Certification in grief recovery specialty and edu-therapy has provided me with additional information; however, it is the lessons that I have learned around the support group table that reinforce my belief that we need to share. Although my accounts are not based on an exhaustive study, what you will read is based on approximately eight hundred group participants. I consider myself blessed as well as better informed after having met and listened to people reaching out, hoping to make sense of this trek through loss. Some fared better than others as they returned week after week to share painful emotions. Some could not, through no fault of their own. Facing grief is hard work, and as humans, we sometimes put off the effort in hope that the pain will dissipate. We bury our feelings. We feel embarrassed to share our feelings as we associate sad emotions with weakness. We convince ourselves that we will recover in time. Sadly, time alone does not heal.

For those of you who persevered in group, I applaud you. You are my evidence that with support and understanding, we can move one another away from bitter toward better.

Reading this book will not take your grief away, but it is my hope that it will provide you with the assurance that you are normal and that as in most valleys of grief, you will discover nuggets of peace that will add to your inner strength.

The Grief Journey

Losing someone you love is a life-changing event. If this is your experience at this moment, I am not sharing something that you don't already know. Emotions become stripped bare, and depending on the choices you make, you will become strengthened or weakened by the process. If you feel that nobody else has experienced such confusion, you are right. If you feel that every other griever must have felt what you are feeling right now, you are right. Whatever you are feeling is right. If you feel nothing at all, know that that is also right.

In his short film *Matthew,* Rob Bell talks about the loss of a dear younger friend whom he looked after and mentored while he was going through university. In expressing his profound sense of loss, he shares his innermost feelings and offers this advice to the viewer: "Whatever you are feeling, it's OK. It's OK."

Our adopted practice of burying grief has created expectations that humans cannot uphold themselves without the support of others.

The grief journey is a natural part of life. Loss triggers physical, emotional, and spiritual responses. The changes accompanying these responses often create unexpected feelings that lead to confusion and exhaustion. Our society has a tendency to minimize emotions associated with loss, thereby creating delays and outright obstacles to recovery.

In the 1960s, my community saw a shift to viewing the deceased in funeral homes, decreasing exposure to the loved one lying in the casket in the home as family gathered for a minimum of three days and three nights. I recall a wreath being placed on the outside of a home where a death had occurred. Grievers, women in particular, wore black clothing for up to a year. The community acknowledged the loss by visiting, bringing food, and sharing stories, while some stayed with family members overnight as the body was never left alone.

Death was not taboo. Support was offered and accepted. Grieving was a normal part of life. When did we decide to shield children from death? Was it when we felt they could be uncomfortable in a funeral home? Was it when antibiotics and other medical cures created the illusion that death could be avoided? Or was it when we stopped having honest conversations about the reality of life? There will be times in life when everyone will experience loss and grief.

Grief is not limited to the loss of a loved one. Life will bring both unanticipated and planned changes that will disrupt the familiar routine, creating a response and a process that must be experienced in order to recover and resume activities deemed to be our normal. That first puppy love that goes sour, loss of a friendship, loss of a pet, and loss of self-esteem perpetuated by unkind words or disapproval are a few examples of loss.

Loss of innocence, especially if resulting from a sexual interference and/or assault, creates huge obstacles in navigating through the grief journey. Victims of these crimes require professional counseling in order to return to a healthy life experience.

Loss of income is often overlooked as the cause of grief as individuals busy themselves with more pressing issues, such as covering the financial debt or finding new sources of revenue. One group participant presented a change in work responsibility as an insidious loss. After finding gratification as a nurse, new policies added the role of team member in medically assisted suicide to her job description. Changes in sleep patterns and eating habits, headaches, and questioning her role as a parent were some symptoms that alerted her to feelings of loss. Once she understood that she was questioning the limits of her compassion for her patients, she was able to identify a personal loss that she needed to address. She became the catalyst that led team discussions. The group was able to address the silent emotional dilemma that others were carrying and provided support to one another.

The overly used caregiver burnout diagnosis is not cured by a stress leave when the underlying issue is grief. There are many reasons that an individual may suffer through loss and grief. Sometimes, even the griever may not recognize his/her symptoms as being grief related until past events are explored and the question, When did your symptom first present itself? is asked.

During an educational session on loss, one participant reported that the sale of the family home following the death of her parents was a huge and unexpected loss for her. A sense of familiarity and comfort eluded her even while in her own personal space. Others reported that it was a relief for them when the family home was sold; it provided them with a sense of closure.

One lady came to group with the intention of offering support to those who were grieving. She embraced her work as a counselor and devoted hours exceeding her assigned work time. The gratification she experienced through helping others motivated her to do more, see more clients, and seek more professional success. Through reflective exercises, she found what she described as an aha moment, saying, "I am grieving the loss of personal time. *That* is what is making me feel tired. I miss my joy!" She added that she had been too busy to identify this loss.

A temporary health issue can affect our response to normal activities of daily living. I am extremely reclusive and cranky whenever I have a bad cold or a simple influenza. I have tried to imagine the permanent loss of health. I cannot.

Losses that are not readily acknowledged by those around us make us feel misunderstood and dismissed and limit our access to support from loved ones. Losses that we do not acknowledge limit our access to our inner strength. Do not confuse what I am saying with the need to be strong. I am referring to the need to listen to our inner voice and access the wisdom within—that place that has too often been silenced by learned myths and self-imposed misguided expectations. Healing must begin from within.

Research supports that the body has an initial period, referred to as a buffer zone, following loss when numbness sets in. Group participants often expressed going through the funeral on automatic pilot, surrounded by a vague sense of activities and people around them. As weeks pass by, a new awareness and reality compounded by a withdrawal of support systems may feel like an emotional regression.

In the late 1960s, my generation was embracing the work of Elizabeth Kübler-Ross and her identification of the stages of dying—denial, anger, bargaining, depression, and acceptance. Within the nursing classroom, we happily chatted about these five stages as new discoveries in supporting dying patients and their families. Physicians in my small training hospital mumbled medical jargon on a fast exit from the bedside on their way to writing orders for sedatives and pain medications. Death was safely escorted to funeral homes with scheduled visiting hours. The word *dead* was carefully replaced with *departed* or *passed away*. Surely the pain associated with the death of a loved one could be buried along with the deceased.

It would be years later that I clued in that many group participants were expressing confusion around the stages of grief. Some would say "I have never felt anger" or "I am sad sometimes, but I don't think I'm depressed" or "Obviously, I'm not grieving normally." Too often, I have heard these words: "I am not normal." Others shared, "My friends tell me that I need to move on, but I don't know how."

I revisited the work of Kübler-Ross and discovered that she had never intended the stages to be intended for grievers. The five stages are about the person who is dying. There is no pattern to follow. Only the griever knows their journey. Each response is based on the meaning of the relationship between the deceased and the griever.

Years ago, I began compiling some comments expressed by grievers, including the following:

> "Losing someone you love cannot be this hard. If it was, somebody would have said so."

"I was feeling something like I had never felt before. I knew I was not thinking right."

"For months and months, I felt nothing. Just numb."

"I have this junk in the middle of my chest. It gets in the way of talking, eating, and sometimes, breathing. Sounds funny, but talking about it seems to take my mind off of it."

"I was not prepared for the exhaustion."

"Everything in the world is different. I have been at my workplace for twenty-eight years. I recently returned to work, and nothing is the same. Everything is different. I just realized it's me that's different."

"The third week was the worst. After everyone went back to their own lives."

"I feel like I swallowed a bunch of toonies. My stomach is full and heavy. Every time I can talk about it, some of those toonies come out."

"I kissed his picture. The glass was so cold. It frightened me."

"I remember all the bad things. They are in my head over and over again, about the call and not being able to hold her that one last time."

"I feel like I'm in a deep, cold concrete well, protected for now, and there are cracks in the walls that are letting things in, and I'm afraid of what those things are."

"It is just unbearable at times."

"I feel like I should cry! Why can't I cry?"

"I find myself at the bottom of a deep well, and occasionally, I can look up and see the light. I climb on one rung, sometimes two or three, and then I fall to the bottom again."

"I don't want to feel better. I don't want to forget her. What if I forget her voice?"

"I hate Christmas lights now. They remind me of that last ambulance ride. A lot of houses were decorated along the way."

"I just want to scream."

"I used to believe in God. Now I'm not so sure."

"I can be in a crowd and still feel so all alone."

"I am not judging anyone or myself, but I am feeling very vulnerable right now. My grief is bogging me down. I am most out of place in this present moment."

"I don't like being by myself. I'm OK if people are around me."

"What's the point of all the things we do on a daily basis? What does anything matter?"

The topic of depression can be a confusing one. What is the difference between sadness and depression? Depression is defined as a general sadness with loss of interest in normal activities of daily living. Some participants told of clothes mildewing in the clothes dryer and lacking the motivation to complete the task. Some shared days when they didn't want to shower or leave the house. One lady shared that she could manage tasks during the daytime but had to sit in darkness as the day turned into night. Despite the concern (and comments) from the neighbors, this was her grief journey. This kind of sadness/depression is a normal response to a significant loss for many individuals. It is only when these feelings persist for weeks without improvement that a clinical depression may be developing and counseling and short-term use of medications should be considered.

Physiological responses such as headaches, abdominal discomfort, or unusual fatigue are often blamed on a different cause than the grief process. Research supports evidence that grief stimulates the secretion of chemicals and hormones that directly impact the digestive tract, immune system, and brain. Many group participants have shared they visited emergency rooms with symptoms of chest pain, shortness of breath, palpitations, and other physiological symptoms that were not substantiated by medical investigations. It is not unusual to experience changes in appetite. Although some participants admitted to eating less, some did say they were eating foods that they would not have chosen before.

One gentleman confessed that he was eating cold beans out of the can, adding it was "simpler and fewer dishes." Some admitted to eating in excess. Other physical symptoms included low energy and general weakness that some explained as a loss of strength. Neck tension, abdominal discomfort, headaches, and disruptions in sleep were common physical complaints. For some, a change in libido did create problems between couples, as one sought the added comfort of sexual intimacy, and the other lost all interest in sex. Some felt guilty enjoying any pleasure while grieving and often misinterpreted enjoyment as being insensitive to the loss. Having an understanding of how people process grief in different ways, although helpful, was not always effective in keeping couples monogamous. Loss of pleasure also extended to those places, and activities that once were enjoyed are no longer providing any joy, peace, or sense of security.

Participants said they expected to be sad. However, they were surprised at their new emotions of anxiety, fear, and panic, and they worried that they would stay in this emotional state. Hearing others express the same feelings was a huge part of their relief and hopes of moving forward. Some shared that they felt they were being punished by losing the person they loved, identifying feelings of low self-esteem. Again, shared conversations about these common emotions that many tend to hide while grieving encouraged many. Over and over again, I heard, "Maybe I'm not crazy." It is not a matter of coping better, as it is an understanding that it is a process we must travel through as our healing begins.

Grief is not a rational journey. It is the journey of a broken heart.

When Jearim was three-and-a-half years old, he had to stay with his grandparents while both his parents were on military assignments. While FaceTiming with them, he said, "I miss you. My heart hurts." Children know that grief is not resolved by intellect. Children know about sharing and seeking support. It is the expectation that adults often place on themselves that prolongs the journey.

Emotional responses such as sadness, loneliness, anxiety, and anger are common and generally expected. What may not be expected is the emotional conflict as negative and positive feelings collide. A feeling of relief may be superimposed on a feeling of abandonment just as a feeling of freedom can be consumed by feelings of guilt. It is important to recognize the ambush of different emotions coming all at once as being part of the grief process.

Spirituality includes one's faith, but it is much more than that. Our spirituality is the essence of who we are and the foundation of what provides us with our strength, our peace, and our security. Expect your spirit to be affected by grief. It is not unusual for grief to rob a person of their inner peace, even in the most faithful.

There was one man who arrived to grief group and stated that he could not participate while the cross of Jesus Christ hung on the wall. He explained that he did not believe there was a God. I briefly struggled with the best response to his discomfort, and with the group looking to me for action, I chose to take the cross down. That man returned to all the sessions, and then I started seeing him as a regular attender in church. There are those who find their faith in the midst of grief.

Participants have expressed various changes in their spirituality:

> "I used to love going to the beach. Now it's just a lonely place."

"Music was always my mood lifter. Now all music just makes me cry."

"I used to love being with my friends. Now I just want to be alone."

As unique and individual as we humans are, those who are grieving follow a fairly common path, and it is in identifying and sharing the obstacles that we can facilitate what is one of the most arduous journeys life asks us to embark on. There are some who will try to lead your path, but it is you who must guard and manage your little steps. Listen to your inner voice and do what you need within healthy parameters. Your need for sleep, for food, for time alone, and for tears—this time is about you. Choose without apology to be with persons who do not judge you and give you unwanted advice but who let you grieve in your own way.

In the upheaval of such drastic changes, you are absolutely normal if you are feeling numb, confused, fatigued, and overwhelmed.

Animals also show signs of grief. Research has identified evidence of wild animals grieving. Storytellers also have personal accounts of altered behavior in pets following the death of a person. I have a personal story of my own.

My second husband's dog, Bud, was his constant companion. George's disability robbed him of his ability to maintain employment, and so man and dog spent their days together while I worked. On the day that George died, Bud retreated under the table and slowed his step considerably, even when called to his food. He wandered to the door and the window repeatedly only to eventually return to his space, eyes down. I was no help to the dog. Much to the dismay of family and friends, I found a young boy who wanted Bud, and I gave him away. The opinion I received from some well-intended individuals and some strongly opinionated individuals was that I was being mean to Bud and that I would regret it. I got it.

Some of the negativity came from dog owners, a different breed all of their own. I never did regret my decision. Bud needed a person who would provide him with love again. With my schedule, that person was not going to be me. I met Bud and his new owner months later. The dog was happy to see me. My decision was upheld by the wagging of his tail as they walked away. The boy's big smile and his words "You can't have him back" warmed my heart. I am in no way suggesting that you give pets away, but I am suggesting that pets need to be in the care of persons who provide them with the attention they need.

Miscarriage and Abortion

Mothers who miscarry know how deep the loss and heavy the grief that follows. Family often does not realize the attachment mother has already formed with the new life within and, in an effort to comfort, too often express sentiments that do not acknowledge her feelings. "You will conceive again" and "It may have been for the best if the baby was not healthy" are comments that can prove hurtful and discourage the mother from sharing her pain. The loss of a dream is directly connected to the loss of a pregnancy. Regardless of how advanced the pregnancy, the mother will grieve based on her journey, her expectations, and her attachment.

A pastor shared with me how he could not understand his inability to console his wife after a miscarriage. "I keep telling her we will have another baby, but she does not want to hear that!" He admitted never having thought to acknowledge her feelings about their loss. Once he understood, he said he could see her point of view and that he would not dismiss her feelings. The old adage of "You don't need to fix it, you just need to listen." Acknowledging someone's grief is most important.

Abortion is another misunderstood loss often judged as an irresponsible action on the part of the mother. Mental health issues, pressure from loved ones, financial burdens, and unwanted impregnation are some of the underlying reasons that form the decision to terminate a pregnancy. Judging is never supportive. Years ago, I was caring for a middle-aged woman whom I knew. She had been pressured to abort her teenage pregnancy. She shared that she had eventually agreed to the decision as it would protect her family from shame, and she also felt that she was too young to have a baby. She could have another baby when she was older and married. It saddened me to finally hear her side of the story. She had never conceived again, and throughout her life, whenever she saw a child, she thought of the child she never had. What would he or she look like? She would see children of the age her child would have been, and she would feel the excruciating pain of loss. Regret, guilt, silence—three heavy burdens to carry along with the feeling that some still judged her.

Thankfully, I was never pressured to have an abortion. But I could have been . . .

My mother died two weeks before my graduation from nursing. Two months after her death, I had to tell them that I, the unmarried Catholic girl, was pregnant. Some of them did not take it well. Well, they were grieving, and they were not too fond of the English-speaking boyfriend. I had two choices: (1) be admitted to the Home of the Guardian Angel in the province's capital city three hours away, where the baby would be delivered and kept there until transferred to the nearby orphanage or (2) disappoint my family who may or may not choose to speak to me ever again.

Some did not attend the wedding, but forty-eight years later, Dan is well loved and admired by the entire family. He knows the story and has told me repeatedly, "I'm glad you kept me." We laugh about that now.

DIVORCE

Divorce presents enormous loss for both partners, regardless of who initiates it. Support is often limited as advice is often judgmental, with comments of being better off and/or finding somebody better. What is overlooked is that people marry with hopes of staying happy. My marriage was what I wanted more than anything in the world. I had zero empathy for divorcing couples and admittedly felt some hostility toward adults who would tear the family apart. My logic was that if people could decide to marry, they could certainly decide to reconcile.

I had the pleasure of working with an older lady who shared my views. After I found myself in an unhappy relationship, I gained some understanding into why people divorce. Needless to say, my colleague verbalized her opposition to my decision. After I met her husband, I understood her reasoning. Jim was one of the kindest, supportive men I have ever met, visibly in love with his wife of many years. She obviously believed that all husbands were like hers.

We need to surround ourselves with people who love us. Sometimes, in busy lifestyles, we forget to send loving energy to one another. Love that is not nurtured will not grow. I created an idea for myself that marriage itself was a fertile ground where romantic love would flourish. I was planting seeds of expectation, while my husband was tangled in weeds of married life, fatherhood, and working at two jobs. I knew I was feeling as though I was running from one task to another, but it was not until a brave friend pointed out that she missed my joy. Another pointed out that if I was unhappy, those feelings would be felt by the ones I loved. If I felt joy, the same would apply.

Our solution was to have another baby. Andy was born premature, but once he was finally home from the hospital, our family was happy again. For the next five years, we worked hard; and as work replaced family time, we struggled, we disagreed, and we fought. My husband shared that he had been seeking the attention of other women while I was away to work-related meetings. I kept my disappointment to myself as I was afraid that he might leave. Those hidden emotions grew into resentment, and before long, I was looking elsewhere as well. It was ten years later when we were able to admit our feelings and had an honest conversation about the marriage. He shared that my silence was an indication to him that I no longer cared. I learned a valuable lesson. I believe he did as well. After our divorce, I no longer experienced recurrent pneumonias, and he no longer developed hives. We had been married for eleven years. Some family members expressed that they were not surprised that the marriage did not last, while others could not believe I wanted a divorce as we, to paraphrase their words, appeared happy, he didn't hit me, and he was a good provider.

In 1980, divorce was uncommon in my community. As it was my idea, I carried the blame for the decision. I have a recollection of my oldest son coming home from school, happy that he had met one boy whose parents were also divorced. Fast-forward to 1987, and my stepson told a story about this poor kid in his classroom who only had one set of parents and missed out on double gifts at Christmas time.

On that first Christmas after our separation, my husband wanted the boys with him on Christmas Eve and on Christmas morning. He was settled in a home with his new love, and I was still living by myself; however, I was seeing someone. I decided to meet George for breakfast on Christmas day, and we drove down that long driveway to pick up my sons. They were ten and five years old. George drove, and I went to the door of the house. My husband stepped out of the house with a shotgun pointed at the car. He was yelling and threatening to shoot the gun. I left without the boys and returned later by myself to pick them up and try to celebrate Christmas. The years that followed were difficult, especially after I married George. Those were distressing years for everyone with no possible reconciliation in sight. The boys were living in two separate families who did not communicate with each other. That first connection was not easy, but the time came for us to support our sons as parents should. The two couples agreed to meet and plan how we could be civil in order to attend our son's graduation from dentistry.

I recall his father saying, "I feel as though I am being led to a slaughter" as he and his wife entered our home. My ex and current husband were able to reconcile. I gained a lot of respect for my first husband when, in time, he shared with both our sons that the divorce was not only my fault. He was honest with them about the role that he had played in the collapse of our marriage. Our sons, thankfully, were able to see both their parents and their new spouses get along and socialize. We enjoyed numerous family events, shared meals, and frequently went to camping trips together. Was the journey easy? Absolutely not. Was it worth the efforts? Absolutely yes!

Both my sons married twice, and both divorced twice. There were difficult years with heartbreak, financial setbacks, weekly separation from one child, legal appointments, and all the associated hardships of divorce. Throughout their struggles, I often questioned my parental example in keeping a marriage together no matter what. Then I would recall the peace I felt when home was a happy place to land and not a place for arguments to flourish. Occasionally, some so-called friends would remind me what a poor example I had been to my sons, and I would recall the naive insight that I once held through ignorance. Today, I am happy to see both my sons married to women who make them smile. I appreciate how they are both quick to complement their wives.

Research shows that divorce has a longer recovery phase than death. Participants in my divorce care groups often stated that guilt and feedback from family and friends interfered with their freedom to express their true feelings. One participant had what she referred to as an aha moment. She said, "After he left, I kept trying to convince myself that I was better off without him. I just realized now that I have been lying to myself and saying things that my friends were comfortable hearing." Without an opportunity to have feelings acknowledged, the grief journey is delayed. Self-talk that supports the opinions of others rather than being honest about our feelings is never helpful.

Within my divorce group, there was a large consensus when one lady expressed that men are quick to leave older wives for younger women. One gentleman explained that he had made the decision to end their marriage after he and his wife stopped communicating. Despite marriage counseling, they were not able to regain the friendship and closeness they once had. "The relationship fell apart long before we separated," he said, "and I am devastated!" The group provided a safe space for both genders to acknowledge loss and to consider myths that may affect our decision-making.

One lady shared this: "It's like my girlfriend said, 'Once a cheater, always a cheater,' so I would never take him back if I were you." She admitted nobody had ever asked her if she loved him, wanted him back, and could forgive him. Fortunately, she listened to her own advice. Years later, they are a loving family, raising two wonderful children. Forgiveness does not mean forgetting. It simply means that we all make mistakes, and sometimes, struggling toward solutions together makes us stronger.

In her book *Falling Apart in One Piece* (Simon & Schuster), Stacy Morrison outlines the hellish journey of divorce and leads the reader into exploring expectations based on ideas in our heads as opposed to communicating with a spouse. She tells a story worth reading.

WHAT TO SAY AND
WHAT NOT TO SAY

The most common (well-intended) question grievers often get is, How are you doing? "I'm OK" is the most common answer, but what many group participants shared as what they would like to say is, "How in the hell do you think I'm doing? My loved one is dead!"

The second most common response to "How are you doing?" is "Not so good." Regrettably, that answer will often get a response that does not acknowledge the honest response. Such answers include the following:

1. "Give it time."
2. "Find something to do to take your mind off of it."
3. "Be thankful you have another son."
4. "The living must go on."
5. "You are young and pretty. You will find someone else."
6. "He/she is in God's arms now."

Although the last statement may be truthful, the griever would rather have their loved one here with them on earth.

One comment that brought some laughter to the group was, "I know exactly how you feel. My cat died, and I found that so hard!" This comment was made to a recently widowed lady after forty years of being happily married. She admitted that the absurdity of this comment brought her some relief, and she added, "I love retelling it!" I have no doubt that the love between this woman and her cat had created a huge loss and grief. However, when she shifted the focus from the griever to her experience, she was not allowing the opportunity for expression. Although such dialogue is well intended, it does nothing to support the griever.

Often, I have heard people say, "I just don't know what to say to a person who is grieving." My response is simple: "You just said it." "I don't know what to say" is an honest and caring sentiment to share with a griever. Other helpful sentiments are as follows:

1. "Do you want to talk about it?"
2. "I have no idea what you are going through, but I would like to support you."
3. "Would you like to tell me what happened?"

Many participants were pleased to hear a memorable story about the person who died. What is important to remember is what *not* to say. Do *not* tell them what makes *you* feel better. Do not dismiss what the person is saying by offering what you think is a solution. Do not assume that the person is feeling as bad as you think they should be by adding drama, tears, and descriptive scenarios about their loss.

Several months after my husband had died, I was at the post office, and a known acquaintance, whom I had not seen in years, approached me with arms extended for a hug and a sad, stricken face and a loud voice saying, "Oh, I heard you lost your husband!" Her outburst annoyed me rather than comforted me. My response that I shall blame on my grief-induced emotions was, "I did not lose him. He died. I know exactly where he is!" Rude? Definitely yes. Am I making apologies for that retort? No.

Even with the best intentions of saying what is appropriate, sometimes you miss the mark. My introduction to the English language began in grade 6 as I was brought up French Acadian. At age thirteen, I traveled to Boston where I was introduced to my recently widowed cousin. I extended my hand and mumbled "My congratulations" instead of "My condolences." The faux pas brought much-needed laughter to the griever and those within earshot. I do not recommend that you use this approach.

When you cannot find the words, it is perfectly acceptable to say nothing. On a personal note, I recall being tired of the many "I'm sorry for your loss" as I stood in a reception line by my husband's casket. I do recall those who were present and offered a hug. No words.

Group participants have shared similar stories. Unless you know the person and you are truly sorry for their loss, saying these words with sincerity, accompanied by time to listen, can be meaningful. If you are just repeating what you have heard others saying, "I'm sorry for your loss" holds little value. It is difficult for a griever to accept meaningless words from so many people following a loss.

Canadian Idol (season 3) singer-songwriter Rex Goudie sings a meaningful verse that I feel captures the emotions of many grievers:

> A tide inside your heart
> Keeps rising in the dark
> Surrounds you like an ocean
> And you can't keep from going under.

SUICIDE

"I have thoughts of killing myself so this pain will end." A lot of grievers think about suicide. It does not mean that they intend to act on their thoughts. What if you are talking to a griever, and they share that they are feeling like they want to die? Even contemplating suicide? That is perfectly OK too.

There was a very brave woman in group who had lost her son, and she offered that her suicidal thoughts were scaring her. After listening to her story, I asked the group if anyone else had these thoughts. A second person in the group quickly offered that this was a constant thought of hers soon after her loss, but now a few months into her journey, she was OK letting the emotion come and pass. A third participant who had been quietly listening looked up and spoke. She was on leave from the mental health unit to attend class after being hospitalized for a suicide attempt, and the sharing provided an opportunity for her to share honestly and to be listened to without judgment. Sometimes, normalizing our feelings is the best therapy we can get. Healing conversations occurred frequently as the groups spent time together and developed a sense of trust.

The topic of suicide and the stigma that is still attached to it continues to compound grief associated with a death by suicide. Overwhelming guilt often complicates all the emotions associated with losing a loved one. Sudden death holds its own added component of shock and disbelief. The what-ifs can create never-ending feelings of despair. For a few who have helplessly watched a loved one struggle with mental illness and/or addiction, suicide can bring conflicting emotions of relief and sadness.

The majority of suicide grievers who have attended my support group arrived with a limited view of suicide. Most saw it as preventable, and many felt that they could have done more to save that life. That, in itself, is a heavy burden to carry. One young woman in group shared these wise words: "He died from his illness that caused his suicide."

Some of the unhelpful comments are typical of society's limited understanding. They included, "What kind of upbringing did the person have?" "Why didn't someone see this coming?" "Why did they not get counseling for [name of deceased]?"

The guilt loved ones felt was reinforced by the blame that was implied. Ignorance, even if stated with good intention, may serve the speaker but will weaken the griever.

The pain that is the motivator for a person to choose death over life is only known to the person who commits suicide. There is no clear answer to the causes of suicide, regardless of the identifiable common characteristics of persons choosing to die. As much speculation as survivors have, many take their deep-rooted reasons to the grave.

Statistics Canada reported a rate of 11.5 suicides per 100,000 persons in 2009 in all age groups. My impression, based on media reporting, has been that the youth and the elderly are at a higher risk, although statistics report ages forty to fifty-nine as the highest category. The fluctuation rates since 1950 depicts a rise in the 1970s, highest in the 1980s, and dropping toward the year 2000. In 2012, suicide was ranked as the ninth leading cause of death in Canada and tenth in the United States.

Suicide has been with us throughout history and continues to plague humanity. Statistics are alarming, but for suicide survivors, it is a valuable fact in knowing that others share in the devastating fallout. There is no magic fix in recovering from a loved one's suicide. What I remind my grievers is that two obstacles will slow or even abort recovery: (1) believing the opinions others hold about our grief and (2) the negative myths and thoughts we tell ourselves.

As with any other loss, healing begins in knowing that we are the only one who can take the steps toward recovery. We must acknowledge the emotions. We must share our emotions. We must expect meaning in our life to return.

Having some insight into what other families have experienced after a family suicide can provide some guidance into this lonely and difficult time of life and loss. One of the books that I recommend is *Andrew, You Died Too Soon*, written by Corinne Chilstrom, a Christian mother whose son committed suicide. The book is published by Ausburg Fortress in 1993.

One personal story I shall never forget begins with a telephone call as I was ready to leave the house for a three-hour drive to a meeting. My Mother's Day flower bouquet was still fresh on the table. A sad-sounding voice asked me if I did any counseling. I said no, as I only facilitated group discussions, but asked her why. She shared that her spouse had died from suicide, and she was hoping she could talk to someone. I decided to postpone my drive as it was obvious that she was reaching out. I could visit, and I could listen. I grabbed a rose from my bouquet and drove to her home. After listening to her story, we agreed to meet again. On my way out the door, she asked me if I was a religious person. She explained that a family member had told her to pray to Saint Theresa, and if she smelled a rose or received a rose, she would know her prayers were answered.

I was working at a nursing home in those days, and I shared this story with a group of the elderly residents. One lady immediately wheeled herself to her room and returned with a mass card depicting the full story of Saint Theresa. She read to those gathered the story of Saint Theresa who died from tuberculosis at a young age and devoted herself to doing good on earth once she entered her heavenly home. Blessing recipients would know this through her shower of roses.

The Death of a Child

The death of a child is an unimaginable loss with no peace in sight. We expect our grandparents to die, and we expect our parents to die before we do. Statistically, women outlive men, and so we are more likely to expect the loss of a spouse. We are not created to expect that our children will die before we do. As one grieving mother shared in group, "When our parents die, we are orphans. The death of a spouse makes us a widow or widower. With the death of a child, there are no words."

My experience with grieving parents is limited. I have been acquainted with two families who have both lost a young child in car accidents while the parent was driving. I have observed a strong faith expressed in their kindness and love shown to those around them. I have not discussed their journey with either family. I have only been impressed. I cannot imagine the pain of losing a child or a grandchild.

Several years ago, I was astonished when five couples who had all lost an adult child individually signed up for the support group. These parents did not know one another, but the support they could offer one another was beyond what I could have imagined.

Support sometimes comes from persons we do not expect to carry us through loss. A family was devastated over the accidental death of their toddler. The grandmother was a resident at the nursing home I managed as she had become too frail to care for herself. The grieving family worried that this tragedy would be too much for their grandmother to bear and that, in their words, her heart might give out. Grandmother became their strength, explaining that "we are born, we live, and we die." I clearly recall her words: "Only God knows when we will be born and when we will die, and together, we will get through this." And together they did with frequent visits and a renewed purpose for this wise and loving grandmother.

In sharing Leo Buscaglia's book *The Fall of Freddie the Leaf*, one grandmother told me that this story of the leaf cycle eased her grief while providing her with a story to share with her surviving grandchildren.

I encourage parents to choose carefully if signing on to bereaved parents support groups online as some groups share unsettling language and expressions of blame and hate that are not conducive to healing. I recommend published books of parents' personal accounts.

JOURNALING

I was not always a believer in journaling. Today, I advocate journaling as I have known the benefits it offered me after my husband's death. I have also been privy to many accounts of release of emotions from persons who took up the task. I intentionally use the word *task* as only the griever knows that any new activity is daunting in the midst of grief. I strongly urge them, and you, to try. I like to provide a few suggestions for journaling as I know the blank space my brain travels to when trying to put pen to paper. If the person you loved was sitting in front of you, what might you say to them? Begin there. I learned to journal first thing in the morning when my head is distanced from what the world offered me yesterday. I do not concern myself with spelling or punctuation. I choose a quiet space even if that means getting up when the house is still asleep. If I am lucky, a dream lingers, and I can begin there, catching its tail and running with it. It doesn't matter what I write as long as I write. Eventually, my inner self will come forth and assist me in exploring my true thoughts and introduce me to my true self—the person I was born to become. I like to refer to it as my little voice—my source of peace, security, and strength.

Many have worried that someone else may read their written innermost private thoughts and have avoided journaling for that reason. Burning or shredding a journal will still provide its full benefits.

When I looked back on my writing about the heartache I felt after my husband died, I was grateful that I could revisit the rawness of those emotions. Life will bring pain, and exploring that pain sometimes adds value when joy returns. At the time I was actively journaling, I also appreciated looking back on some days and reading about the progress I was making.

My journal also helped me stay connected with persons who are currently in the midst of their grief. At the time, you just wish to be in a different place, in a different time. Your world feels so unfamiliar. And then, with the support of loved ones and your own determination, you do move forward.

I Hope You Cry

Journaling is therapeutic. Talking is essential. Crying is healing.

One participant summarized her thoughts by saying, "Tears are full of toxins. If you don't let them out, they make you sick on the inside."

Dr. William Frey of the Saint Paul Ramsey Medical Center in Minneapolis states that emotional tears excrete stress hormones. In *The Topography of Tears*, Rose-Flynn Fisher found that tears of laughter and tears of sorrow differ significantly in their chemical content. Tears of sadness are associated with releasing toxins.

We live in our thoughts. The behavior we learned as children plus our present environment form the basis for what we deem acceptable. "Don't cry" is imbedded in most of us. As one participant expressed, "I was often told that if I cried, I would be given something to cry about!"

On some softer notes, I heard these: "People don't want to see those tears" and "Go to your room if you are going to cry." And so we learn at an early age that crying is unacceptable. We learn to suppress our tears.

When I was growing up, I heard that boys who cried were sissies. The boys I grew up with reinforced that sentiment, and both genders mocked any boy who cried in our presence. When the school janitor found Lester hanging from a tree and quickly cut him loose after a rough game of cowboys and Indians, we laughed when Lester cried. The janitor did not laugh.

Dad's wife of more than twenty-five years died when he was fifty-one. Four children still lived at home. He then lost his daughter when she was twenty-six years old. His second wife and two other children died. I never saw dad cry.

My best friend's father was killed when we were in grade school. She was called to the principal's office, a scary action in itself, and did not return to class that day. I heard about the fatal accident the next day, and I was told by my parents and by my teachers that I should not talk about it as it would be upsetting. Years later, I wonder how she felt waiting by herself for someone to pick her up at school with no friends to share her emotions—nobody to acknowledge her enormous loss in the ensuing months and perhaps years.

Regrettably, I recently heard a school teacher tell her young student not to mention that someone had died as it might make them sad, and they might cry. Kids are smart. Her response was "Isn't he already sad?"

I was at the funeral parlor waiting in line to pay my respects to the deceased. My sister was kneeling at the casket when this cute, bouncy four-year-old moved in. My well-intentioned sister smiled at the child and said, "She's sleeping." The four-year-old responded, "Ahh, no, she's dead!"

A school teacher had to inform the classroom that their classmate had died in a house fire and was fighting back her tears. Choosing the right approach and the right words seemed insufficient until one seven-year-old classmate responded with, "I think we should have a moment of silence." Children grieve differently from adults and can often be the ones who bring practical insight and offer comforting words.

The first man I saw cry was my husband George after his grandmother died. He was hiding on the outside deck and apologized for his tears. I was moved and felt enormous love for him in that moment. I saw the love he held for his grandmother and felt sad he could not cry unashamedly.

Many individuals have shared that they do not want to cry in front of their children. Some reasons include these: they don't want to introduce more sadness, they want them to feel secure, they want them to know Mommy/

Daddy are in control, they don't want to think about things that may make them cry, and they want them to think about only happy thoughts. Think about what message we are sending to our kids. The question is, What will happen if we cry with our children? Our tear ducts provide a release for our emotions. Honesty about feelings, all feelings, is healthy. When we know better, we do better, so cry in front of your children and grandchildren and all the little people. Just explain why you are sad and reassure that it's OK to be sad sometimes. When we blindly protect children from disappointments and tragedies of life, we rob them of the opportunity to solve problems and develop coping skills. Crying together as a family or with friends allows for acknowledgment of feelings. And yet how often do we hear "She/he is not doing well" associated with a person crying?

Not everybody sheds tears easily. If you are that type of person, it does not mean you are not grieving properly. It does not indicate that you hold a lower level of compassion. What I am saying is that if you feel the urge to cry and choose to hold your tears inside, you are losing an opportunity to release those toxins and feelings from your system. Family members and friends may misinterpret lack of tears as a lack of caring, and regrettably, I have heard hurtful comments among family members accusing others of what they perceive to be cold insensitivity. I have also heard unfound opinions that absence of tears is indicative of an impending mental breakdown.

Only the griever knows their journey, so it is important to respect what others are feeling rather than forming opinions based on what we feel to be truth. We will only move to a common understanding through listening rather than by closing communications with our words.

CHILDREN AND GRIEVING

Children do not grieve the same as adults as they process information with a child's understanding. Research suggests that death cannot be perceived as final until the developmental age of nine to twelve. From the time of our birth, we embark on an earthly learning journey that begins with the sense of parting with objects and with people. A dropped pacifier or Mommy leaving the baby's sight will often trigger an unhappy response. Peekaboo is a fun activity that quickly returns that which is lost, such as a favorite toy, or who is lost, as in the person playing. The concept of loss is experienced long before we can express our thoughts.

An infant will not feel actual grief associated with loss; however, they will respond to the emotions of the caregiver. It is not unusual for a person to share that an infant becomes more upset following a death in the family. Some have expressed that they cannot leave that infant to the care of someone else as they feel guilty, or it would add to the infant's distress. In reality, another caregiver may provide a calmer space, soothing the infant during the parent's grieving journey and giving a break to both mom and infant. Parents, you don't have to do it all.

The preschool years offer a very limited view of death. The concept of mortality is not yet realized. To complicate matters or to ease reality, whichever way you want to look at it, dreams are often blended into waking times.

One recently widowed mom was asked by her four-year-old child why she was sad. She was honest and said that she was sad because she missed

Daddy. The child walked up to her, looked into her eyes, and explained that Daddy was right there, sitting in heaven and chatting with his friend. That childlike assurance uplifted her.

The preschool years reinforce the concept of self-centeredness as all needs are met. A death in the family may be perceived as an inconvenience to the child. "But you said I could go to my friend's house. I don't want to go to a stupid funeral home!" are difficult words to hear. Remember that these actions reflect a child's comprehension and not a lack of compassion.

Should you bring a child to a funeral home? The answer depends on the child and on the circumstances. First, the child has to be told what to expect in terms he/she can understand. Be patient in waiting for questions the child may pose. It is suggested to then ask the child if he/she would like to go. It is always a good idea to bring the child into the funeral home before too many adults create excess stimulation. An adult should stay with the child until it is time to leave.

The year was 1959. It was the middle of the afternoon, yet we were allowed to play indoors. Mom underestimated the curiosity she aroused by pulling down the dark-green kitchen window shade. In a crowded kitchen filled with nine children excited over homemade fudge, it was not difficult to slip away and not be missed. Safe at the upstairs bedroom window, I watched, bewildered as a long black car, one like I had never seen before, backed to the front door of Edna's house. I observed a dark-cloth covered cot being placed in the back of the car through one single back door, connecting what should have been the car trunk to the back seat. After that day, Edna's disappearance became a mystery to me as I overheard the adults whispering about death. In 1959, children were not included in conversations about the death of a child. In 2018, the topic of death remains taboo.

As I grew older, my experience with loss was what I consider fortunate. The viewing of the deceased with the body kept in the home allowed ample time to share the sadness, the tears, and the memories, and eventually, the laughter. Children were part of it. I learned at an early age that it is OK to feel sad or mad because eventually glad returns. It was back then that I learned that grief is a family affair. Our parents didn't fix the problem, but they modelled the path to recovery.

The preschool age is also a time of magical thinking: the ability to move the mind to a happier place and time. A magical thinker may also plan how to fix the situation and may offer solutions to the death. It is important to encourage the child to share thoughts and ideas no matter how irrelevant. It is not a time to correct or redirect or explain but to listen.

From ages six to eight, magical thinking gives way to more concrete thinking. The world is seen as black and white, and words are taken literally. "God took Jamie" or "Katie has gone to sleep and is not coming back" will cause confusion and fear. If God took Jamie, then maybe he will come get me too. If I go to sleep, I may never wake up. The bogeyman and ghosts present scary notions within this age group. It is important to acknowledge what the child is feeling as opposed to dismissing his reality. One trick that I used while the kids were in this stage was to use a "magic" spray bottle that prevented these scary characters from returning.

This age can also believe that only old, sick, and bad people die. In the event that none of these apply to the deceased, the child may conclude that the death was caused by a bad person. That idea can lead to the conclusion that maybe they were the bad one who caused the death, especially if they misbehaved or had a misunderstanding with the person who died.

Difficulties in school, inattentiveness at home, disrupted sleep, and health complaints are examples of changes in behavior that indicate the child is struggling with emotions. As children of divorced parents often question if they were the cause of the breakup, it is common for children to fear that they are responsible for other bad things happening. A child may carry this guilt for years as it is felt to be too shameful to admit. Encouraging conversations about the person who has died provides the child an opportunity to share thoughts and feelings. A trusted adult outside the immediate family circle sometimes can be more successful in having the child speak his mind.

Various articles report ages from nine to twelve as being the earliest a child can comprehend that death comes to everyone and that death sometimes has no explanation or warning. This realization is accompanied by an interest in the meaning of life, good and evil, and what happens in the afterlife.

Rural living comes with a dug well and an above-ground well cover. Imagine my surprise finding my son with the heavy cement cover moved to the side, yelling down to see if the devil would answer. Curiosity is the first determinant of great accomplishments. Do not be surprised at how children will seek knowledge.

My ex-husband's daughter spent a lot of time at my home, and she developed a fondness for my new husband. One day, he looked at her and said, "Are you visiting again?" Her eight-year-old face lit up. She looked at me, retorting, "He likes me!" She would often convince him to play with her outdoors. His stroke had left him with partial paralysis of one leg and a contracted arm. One winter day, she convinced him to make snow angels by lying on the ground and extending arms and legs. His arm allowed only a partial extension and a lopsided pattern in the snow. Her honesty in exclaiming that his angel was dumb-looking was a fresh and welcome affirmation of his disability as opposed to persons who pretended not to see. In his journal, he entered these words: "I know people mean well when they try to make me feel better with words or ignoring my disability but most times they don't. They only make me feel worse."

The relationship they developed was precious. When she asked me to visit the cemetery shortly after his death, I was impressed. We had walked in different cemeteries before as that was one of our fun activities along with exploring abandoned houses and pretending ghosts were chasing us back to the car. Still, I thought it was mature of her to want to visit George. Shortly after arriving at the graveside, she blurted, "Do you think he's purple yet?" She had a serious question that she wanted answered, not out of disrespect but out of a child's curious mind. Do not be surprised at what actions or words are expressed by a child who is trying to grasp the meaning of death.

Increasing hormones in the teenage years bring about pleasure-seeking as the world extends beyond the family unit. It is a time of separating family needs from individual needs. Balancing death with living to the fullest can lead to seeking new answers. The lifestyle of those who are risk-takers can become most appealing to this age group as they are fraught with ideas on how to defy death.

I saw a sign that read "Attention teenagers: Move out of the house now while you know more than your parents." At first it reminded me of my teenage children, and quickly, I recalled that it was a generational saying. I moved out of home when I was sixteen, lying about my age to get into nursing school as I wanted to be independent. I had learned all there was to be learned at home or so I thought at the time. The following year, I faced my mother's death. It was a time of being strong and yet being vulnerable. It was a time of being in control and yet needing reassurance. It was a time of being a grown-up while feeling like a lost child. I believe teenagers today feel the same need to be in control while yearning for understanding. Parents can assist by having conversations about the deceased, talking about things that are reminders of the person, including ideas about what the person might say if they were present and introducing related humor while respecting the relationship for the deceased.

We are brought up with the idea that we need to be strong. Strength being compared to "keeping your emotions in check" regardless of the situation. During my RN training, part of our curriculum included professional development. Showing sympathy was taught to be a sign of weak nursing skills. Crying was inappropriate professional behavior.

In 1982, I was called to the bedside of another sister who was dying. Donna had been born with an undiagnosed cognitive impairment, and she had been institutionalized months after my mother's death as she required twenty-four-hour supervision. When Donna took her last breath, the RN at her bedside cried. That honest reaction provided me with more comfort than words ever could have. From that day forward, I realized that compassion is very much a part of helping people heal.

It is as children that we learn to medicate our pain. That first embrace from a loving person, that first taste of a favorite food or drink, that first accomplishment that earned us a reward, or that special gift that lifted our spirits taught us that we can feel better. As we move into adulthood and face bigger losses, we already have chosen those things or places that we can go to in order to feel better. Some choose alcohol as a reward after a hard day's work, while others may choose shopping, or if you are Canadian, a stop for coffee and a treat at Tim Hortons or a workout at the local gym.

All these actions, including gratification from a job well done, are healthy releases.

As we grow older and face times of despair and unbearable emotions, the need to self-medicate is real. That is human nature and does not indicate our weakness, so let's not be hard on ourselves. If we choose to stifle our negative emotions by hiding them from others, it is to be expected that we will seek other opportunities to feel joy. Our healthy habits can become obsessions, a fix to avoid feeling the pain of loss. The trap is to avoid losing our personal power to addictive behaviors. Whenever we choose overeating, drinking in excess, excessive gambling, pornography, or other actions that begin to control our time, we begin to lose sight of what is causing us grief. Initial numbing or avoidance of pain can seem attractive; however, we are only deadening our emotions. The journey may be delayed, but emotional or physical outbursts may resurface at a time that may not be our choosing. While some addictive behaviors may be frowned upon by society, workaholics and fitness junkies who may be avoiding grief may not alert loved ones to their struggles and may not gain the attention they need.

We are at our best and living the life we were intended to live when we are true to ourselves and honest with persons closest to us. When I was struggling with the guilt associated with choosing to divorce my spouse and listening to the well-intended advisers who were reminding me to think of what I would be doing to the children, I was fortunate to hear some useful advice. A colleague of mine drew a tiny dot in the middle of a blank page. Around that dot, he drew one large circle filling the page and a medium-size circle around the dot. I was the dot, and the inner circle was my family and closest friends. The outer circle was people whom I and my family had and would interact with. He wrote out different emotions around the dot to create a visual of how my happiness or frustrations would always influence the people in my life. I could pretend to be happy or choose to be happy. What did my loved ones deserve?

Toward Recovery

The person who is grieving needs to listen to their own little voice rather than to the advice of others.

One widow in our support group expressed it well. She shared that she was often exhausted by the advice she was receiving from friends. "You should find a hobby." "You should volunteer." "You should be thankful for all the years you shared and think about that instead of crying too much."

One day, she responded with, "Is that what you did when your husband died?"

"Ah, well . . . my husband didn't die."

"I didn't think so."

It is not an adviser who gets a person through the journey. It is a listener—one who does not judge or make assumptions. Even if I have lost my husband, I have no idea what another widow is feeling. I do know that whatever they are feeling is perfectly OK.

Thanatologist and author Douglas Smith teaches us that helping others heal requires four components:_authenticity, empathy, unconditional positive regard, and ability to show all three.

Being yourself and being in the moment allows the griever to make that human connection that fosters trust and allows honest communication.

Whenever I speak to nursing students, I remind them that they must introduce themselves. Say your name. Make eye contact. Make yourself approachable. Wear your name tag clearly. Rushing into a conversation telling a person what *your* purpose is and wearing your name tag below your waist will never create an environment of healing.

Having been a patient in hospital, I have experienced that busy nurse who has heightened my anxiety. Thankfully, I have encountered many more who improved my health by administering a compassionate approach along with the treatment.

As opposed to feeling sorry for the person, empathy requires an understanding of the person's journey by imagining what it might feel like to be in their shoes. It is not pity. Regardless of the circumstances that have brought the person to this stage/event in life, in order to assist the person to move toward healing, you must accept where they are without judgment.

When my husband was in his thirties, he was referred to a cardiologist for chest pain. He required a coronary bypass due to advanced arteriosclerosis (clogged arteries). He was a smoker. The lecture we both heard in that doctor's office added insult to the devastating diagnosis. Those words would not cure his smoking habit. Thankfully, the medical profession is leading society into accepting that drug (including nicotine) addiction must be regarded as a health threat requiring serious intervention rather than being dismissed and demoralized as self-inflicted.

Authenticity, empathy, and unconditional positive regard. If we want to make a difference, we need to be open to listening. But first we need to acknowledge the loss. Acknowledge means that we choose to be present. Acknowledge means that we are willing to listen and hear what the person is saying and that we seek to understand what the person needs to share. We encourage more conversation by listening rather than talking. We are willing to hear the worst part of the story. We are willing to be present in the rawness of their emotion even if their words may hurt.

A good friend shared that each time she visited her mom in hospital, she would hear all the bad things her mother was going through. "Some [painful] stuff goes way back, and I have to hear it all. When my brother visits, she puts on a good front to make sure he is OK!" My friend was resentful and hurt. I asked her who she dumped on when she was upset, and she realized it was her husband, the one closest to her heart. Sometimes, as humans, we share our pain with the one we know has the love and the strength to take it and to help us through. That gave her another perspective. My friend's mother died several months later. She was glad she had been there to support her mother. No regrets.

It is not always easy to carry the burden of others, especially when you are grieving. We need to take care of ourselves along the way. Traveling this path, watching a loved one struggle and suffer is exhausting. Sometimes, other persons in the family circle who are affected by the loss add to the demand for support. This reality was routinely expressed in the group by parents and main caregivers. If you are burned out, you cannot be present for someone else. Taking care also means that we need to find activities to replenish our energy and have outlets to express our grief. Whatever attempts we make to seek short-term fixes to medicate our pain only serve as temporary delusional remedies.

I had the privilege of working with and learning from health-care providers and physicians devoted to natural recovery of grief. Antidepressants, anxiolytics, or hypnotics often serve an effective purpose in easing the immediate period following a loss. Some participants in the support group admitted that physicians had prescribed pills to help them relax and/or sleep following their loss and had found the prescriptions most helpful. Some physicians and pharmacists also reported that long-term use of medications is known to mask the symptoms of grief that will resurface once the medications are discontinued. Long-term use can also compromise the function of body organs that detoxify these chemicals. Learning to medicate our pain is part of growing up—from our first boo-boo that qualifies for a kiss to make it all better to that cookie to take our mind off the pain.

One grandmother shared that when her son drowned, she could not talk about it. Whenever she saw his young daughters, she would take them for ice cream. "They mentioned their daddy, but I changed the subject. We made a lot of trips to that ice cream store," she said. Two strong messages emerged from that routine: (1) grief can be remedied and (2) keep your feelings to yourself. Both myths are well accepted in our culture. We pass on beliefs to our younger generation with kind intentions of easing their mind and distracting them from negative emotions. In reality, we are asking people to bury their feelings in ice cream. When we know better, we do better. Recent mental health media attention is changing how we view loss and grief, focusing on the need to talk to express and to share feelings. We still have a long way to go.

Years ago, I had the privilege of hearing a sociologist speak about her visit to Rwanda postgenocide. Most of us cannot conceive of the magnitude of grief permeating that society. She visited a village where the women were creating their own economy by making crafts. Wondering how any semblance of recovery could be possible, she posed the question. One older lady was identified as the leader who had instilled hope in the survivors by providing occasions for everyone to talk about their grief. "We will talk about it."

Keeping busy and distracting ourselves remains a misleading path in avoiding grief. Our intellectual reasoning is supported by what people say: "In time, you will feel better." "Give it time." "Time heals."

Time alone will *never* heal our pain if we bury our emotions. It is a myth that is carried forward from generation to generation. We have all met people who suffered a huge loss years ago, and they cannot let go of the pain. Some have their life on hold, mired in the quagmire of regret, pain, or pity. I believe that those persons who have not recovered have not been given the opportunity to be listened to and acknowledged. We may hear the person who repeatedly relives the emotions of loss while we turn a deaf ear to what is being said. In other instances, we may hear but attempt to redirect what is being said by offering solutions such as "You will feel better in time" or "Give it time." Unless the griever's emotions are acknowledged, the griever may stay stuck in grief.

A young widow was left with two young children after her husband suffered a brain injury and died. The community offered many condolences but regrettably overlaid them with comments such as "You are young, you will marry again" and "You are lucky you have children" and "He is in a good place now" and "You would not want him to live like that." She shared that nobody had ever acknowledged her losses for years, and consequently, she was stuck in her grief for years.

Most of us expect a recovery time if we suffer an injury or have a surgical procedure. We know that a heart attack will slow us down for a considerable amount of time. We offer empathy to persons struck by physical illness, yet we are reluctant to acknowledge persons suffering through loss.

Grieving a loss is an attack on the heart. We cannot intellectualize it away, busy it away, or seek distractions in order to avoid it. It demands a recovery time along with rest and restorative measures. It may be buried, but it will not remain ignored.

Over and over again in group, participants expressed disappointment at not feeling any sense of joy after two, three, and sometimes, more years. They often compared themselves to other grievers: "Others seem to move on. Why can't I?" or "I go to bed with the TV on so I don't have to think about [name]. My friend said that helps him."

Comparing our grief to how others appear to be managing theirs is counterproductive. It creates self-imposed expectations that are based on speculation rather than fact. We don't truly know how the other person is coping. They are on their individual journey, and we are on ours. Minimizing our feelings can slow our recovery process.

Having an understanding of the grief process and taking steps to express our thoughts—be it verbally with a trusted friend or a counselor or writing them down—are all steps toward recovery. A nonjudgmental family member may provide support; however, the emotional tie can lend more sympathy than empathy. The goal is to explore feelings, not quick-fix the problem.

A very caring and loving husband repeatedly told his wife that when she kept talking about their son's death, she was only reliving the nightmare. He continued to encourage her to put it behind her, forget the past. "You are trying to live with the dead," he would say. It was only after she met another mother who had lost her child and who wanted to listen, acknowledge, and share that she could begin to grieve. She shared that she had thought she was losing her mind when in fact, she had lost a piece of her heart. Both mothers had lost a child, but that does not mean that they knew what the other was feeling. What they did share was the need to talk and be heard.

An Individual Journey

Each grief journey is as individual as you are.

My sons suddenly lost their father shortly after his sixtieth birthday. Their dad and I had divorced years before and had thankfully regained a friendly bond.

My youngest son lived away at the time and was sharing his home with his stepsister who had moved to the city following high school. This was his account:

> I learned of my father's death close to midnight while standing outside a coffee shop in Northern Ontario. I received a call on my cell phone, and it was my stepmother on the other end of the line. The words "Your father drowned" still do not make sense to me to this day. He was sixty.
>
> I remember looking up at the stars, and I was lost for a moment in time. I climbed into my truck and began the four-hour drive back home to pick up my teenage sister. What was I going to say to her?
>
> I was separated and on the verge of divorce at the time, and the first person I called was my ex-wife. We cried together, and when I hung up the phone, I punched the dash of my truck several times. This was the first

emotional roller coaster that led me down the road of feeling angry, confused, sad, depressed, guilty, and even suicidal at times.

I thought I was crazy for a while. Until I decided to talk about my inner turmoil with those closest to me, I soon learned that the feelings I had were normal throughout the grief process. Talking openly about how I truly felt was the first step to recovery from extreme emotional outbursts. Other people soon began to talk about their losses and shared their own feelings, which made me feel less alone.

While sharing openly with others was the start for me, talking, reading, and spending time alone in nature helped me a great deal. The woods offered a place where I could reconnect with my dad as we spent some of our best times there. I talked to him a lot, and I still do to this day.

I set new goals to strive for to make my father proud, in that I would not allow his death to be the death of my own life. Physical, mental, and spiritual exercise combined with talking about death as openly as any other subject was key for me to come to terms with his passing.

I was eventually able to use my father's death as a learning tool to motivate me to live my life to the fullest while I still could. I went back to school at age thirty-five, completed two diplomas, and now serve my country in the Canadian Armed Forces some seven years later. I am happily married with two beautiful children, and I often chuckle when I see my dad in my own self as a father. My father's memories take precedence over his death and my own personal loss. The pain is still there, but it is far less that it once was.

Sarah was a group participant who connected months after group had finished. She shared this:

I just wanted to share with you what the last week has been like for me. Since you were there for the beginning, I wanted to include you with the ending. I had a very strange and unexpected thing happen to me. I went to the beach on the anniversary of his death. I literally drew a line in the sand and crossed it. On the other side of the line, the side I was living on for the last year, and the literal side of the line that he drowned on—I said goodbye and let it all go. I sat on my new side of the line, and I felt peace. Since then, after the sadness of that day passed, I have felt a huge weight lifted off me. I think lugging around all that grief and sadness was an emotional ball and chain and was weighing me down.

I will never forget him, but I don't want to be weighed down by the grief and sadness I have been carrying. When I let it all go, left it on the other side of the line, for the first time in a year, I have felt peace and happiness reenter my soul. Freedom, openness. I did not expect this. But letting it all go set me free. For the first time in a year, I feel like myself again. I'm always such a happy positive person, so being sad and grieving, waiting for the dark storm cloud of the looming anniversary to pass, was not my normal self. Now I find I have returned to my pre-his-death self— happy, positive, open, and normal.

I get to be *me* again, and it feels great. I have missed being me. And I do not miss the ball and chain of grief that I have been lugging around. I will remember him not by photographs but by the feeling I have inside of me—the feeling of love we shared before he passed. I don't want to remember the past year. It was hell. I want to remember the feeling he created within. I have been a warrior for the past year. I have battled a war. And I feel I am victorious. My war is over; it's on the other side of the line, and I am not looking back. I see nothing but sunny skies in my future. I like being myself again.

What if I Forget the Person Who Died?

"I don't want to forget the person!" is a common concern. Love keeps the memory alive. Recovery from loss never means we forget. The person may leave us, but the love we shared stays.

In the summer of 2010, I noticed my mind was going back to my sister Alice a lot more than usual. It seemed like something would remind me of her almost on a daily basis. She would have been sixty years old on December 3 of that year. A nagging sense, or Alice, convinced me that I should hold a celebration of her life, but then I thought that may seem weird. I did what most of you would do. I called a friend—my trusted sister-in-law—and asked her if she thought people would think I was crazy.

"They already know you're crazy," Gloria said, "so why not trust your gut?"

I phoned Alice's widower who remarried and told him what I was thinking about. He agreed that it was a good idea, adding, "But I don't want to come." He said he thought it could be good for their son as there had not been too much conversation about his mother. While on the phone, he told his wife of my plan, and she encouraged him to attend. Before he hung up, he said, "Who knows, you may see me there." He was diagnosed with terminal cancer a short time after that phone call, and we held the celebration of Alice's life on the week her husband was buried. Family and friends, some from long ago, gathered, and the focus became what Alice gave us in those short years of her life. I discovered new things about my sister on that day, and my mind returned to rest.

In the summer of 2013, I learned of a young woman who had died after a short illness, leaving behind a husband and teenage children. I vaguely knew her sister as we had shared a large workplace years before. The two sisters had attended a session I facilitated on Alzheimer's disease years before, but my memory of the deceased was blurred. As Christmas season approached, I was becoming more aware of the grief the sister must be feeling. I was experiencing a nagging sense of trying to help in whatever way I could. I mentioned this to a great friend and suggested we consider inviting the sister to our girls' weekend away in January. She totally agreed. We could be sister replacements at least for one weekend. One of the girls decided to bring everyone a small gift. She chose a brooch for the sister, the new girl. Unbeknownst to anyone, the sister had a collection of brooches that she used to wear every day. She had stopped wearing the decorative pins after her sister died. That weekend away with us, she wore her new pin and resumed that practice. That sister continues to be a great friend to all of us. We meet quarterly to sample local cuisine and talk. Whenever she says, "I'm so glad you chose me as a friend," I remind her she had nothing to do with it. It was a message from heaven. We laugh, and then we wonder.

We often overlook the lessons learned within human relationships until we look back and realize the impressions we are left with when the person is no longer there. At first it can be so painful we may think that we will never recover. Talking about the person softens that pain. It is the relationship that is grieved, not the name designation. During a teaching seminar, there was a statement made by a participant that a sudden death was much more difficult to recover from than death following a terminal illness. I was surprised by the strong consensus expressed by the group. By creating different scenarios of the existing relationships with the griever and the person expected to die and the person whose death was sudden, the group was able to grasp that it is only the griever who knows.

One lovely lady comes to mind. She was grieving the loss of her grandmother and would tear up at the mere mention of her name two years within her grief journey. Nobody but her realized the depth of the love she had for her grandmother who had also been her friend and her mother figure. Her mother was living, and friends would often remind her that it was not as though she had lost her mother. Nobody but her knew it would have been less painful to lose her mother.

Another participant shared that her mother died when she was eleven years old. Whenever she shared that fact, she would invariably be met with expressions of regret, accompanied by sad-sounding apologies. She shared that she was not that close to her mother, and if her father had died at that age, she would have felt abandoned. Her dad spent a lot of time with her as her mom's time was spent with seven children, one of whom required twenty-four-hour care. She felt considerably closer to her dad.

A lady married for fifty years was recently widowed. These were her words: "I don't know what to do. Someone told me that I should dispose of his stuff, and someone else said not to. One friend told me I was going to be sad for five years, and another told me I need to find something that I like to do. I was leaving the house every day, and now I'm too tired to go out."

People need to listen to their own little voice and do what feels right for them. There is one hitch in that piece of advice and that is being stuck replaying learned myths of being strong and keeping busy.

GUILT

Guilt over a relationship that could have been better can prove to be an insurmountable obstacle of the grief journey. A parent or loved one that we feel could have loved us more will send waves of regret mixed with the loss, adding to the confusion. Our own actions with a person who has died may leave the void of unfinished business. "I should have been kinder, more understanding, more forgiving . . ." can play repeatedly in our mind, thereby delaying the grief process and compounding our pain. When participants share that they are feeling guilty for a variety of reasons, I often will quietly ask if they intended to cause the person harm. On one occasion, a participant asked to speak to me after class and confessed that she had indeed wished her loved one some harm. Filled with regret, she shared the details. Honesty is one step toward letting go of the guilt. Writing an apology to the person who has died is another step toward recovery. I found that role-playing by having her address me as if I was the deceased to whom she was apologizing brought her a sense of closure. Carrying negative emotions for a lifetime is not an option. It will destroy our sense of well-being and eventually compromise our health.

Another participant admitted being stuck on remembering all the times her deceased mother had treated her badly. Some of her recollections were valid reasons for emotions of anger based on being abandoned. Yet the guilt she felt for having these feelings was consuming her daily thoughts. After writing all the events that caused her so much pain, I encouraged her to use the tool of writing both negative and positive events within the relationship. At first she thought there were no positive things to write, and then she remembered earlier events in her life and attempts her mom had made to reconcile. She was pleased to reach a point in her journey that she could let the negative go and accept that her mother may have done the best she could under her circumstances. Her words were "I feel better knowing I am no longer dishonoring my mother." The pain we hang on to is taking up free rent in our heads. We are only hurting ourselves. Talk about it. Write about it.

I generally tell the group that the topic of guilt takes a minimum of a two-day workshop to explore. Most of us carry guilt of one kind or another. If only we could retitle guilt to mistakes, learn from them, and move on. If only.

There will be a new day that arrives, but as the old is dissolving, the road is very bumpy. The passage is only made easier when we have help along the way.

Whenever I ask a group how many like to help someone, the hands go up. Whenever I ask how many feel comfortable accepting help, the hands move downward. Let somebody help you. Just don't let them tell you how to feel.

GRIEF WORK

On the first week of grief support group, I assign participants the first homework assignment: a template for recording what they are experiencing physically, emotionally, spiritually, and in their social interactions along with a sliding scale rating from poor to improved. I provide them with a folder entitled "My Grief Journey" and add loss and grief-related information on a weekly basis.

I do not ask them to share their responses unless they want to; however, I do explain the benefit of writing as a way of moving emotions. I do suggest that the effort that they make will enhance the value that they will get from our sessions while acknowledging that their energy may not be up to par. Some participants have met me months later and told me they were finally doing the homework.

Other weekly exercises include logging their life-long losses, describing helpful and not-so-helpful actions and/or support that related to their loss, exploring the positive and negative memories with the person they are grieving, and a written and current conversation to the person who has died.

Here is one example of a response from week 2:

> *Physical.* Always tired or could feel good if I could rest.

> *Emotional.* Antsy around public and a bit of a recluse.

Spiritually. New album out from an artist I love. Looking at things a little better.

Relationally. Still a little drone like if people are close. Closed off society.

Overall. A bit better but sort of apathetic.

This tool allows participants to focus on their emotions and allows them to monitor changes as the support group progresses.

One of the exercises focuses on writing the person who has died a letter, sharing emotions and words that were not able to be expressed prior to the death. For some, the idea of saying goodbye seemed too difficult. One very soft-spoken participant shared this reality: "But they [loved ones] have already said goodbye." For those who complete the final evaluation, I am always pleased to see progress. Thankfully, I have never heard otherwise. That in itself motivates me to continue the community support groups.

One aspect of the grief work is related to diet as it plays a huge role. Many participants explain that preparing a nutritious meal only adds to their exhaustion, and besides, they are often not hungry. Some have an increased appetite. Grabbing fast foods and sweets or opening a can of anything is commonplace. Regrettably, an increase in fats, sugar, salt, and carbohydrates contributes to the existing physical discomforts. A rush from a sweet treat will metabolize into low energy. Alcohol has the same effect. A healthy water intake adds to physical well-being; however, during grief, too many trips to the bathroom prove to be a disincentive. Maintaining a well-balanced nutritional diet increases both energy and well-being; however, this is easier said than done. Keeping a nutritional log can prove very helpful. Although it should be obvious, we often do not pay attention to the influence food plays in how we feel. Our body needs proper fuel in order to assist in recovery.

Many participants admitted to keeping busy. Some said it worked well during daytime hour. However, when heads hit the nighttime pillow, emotions generally spilled out—unless delayed again by swallowing medication. Other avoidance practices included eating, gambling, shopping, or surfing the internet.

Loss of pleasure and feeling guilty for enjoying pleasure can cause disinterest in music, sunsets, and other things previously enjoyed. I have often heard the complaint "Well, he doesn't talk under normal circumstances, and he sure is not going to see a therapist!" Regrettably, there remains a stigma associating counseling as being a sign of weakness or an inability to manage your own affairs. Written and honest, loving communication has proven successful in some cases. Go first. Admit the difficulties you are having in hopes of seeking a shared resolution. If we do not share what we are thinking and feeling, we are missing half the information required to move forward as a couple.

Hard work is totally acceptable and often praised in our society. If work becomes a practice used to avoid talking about grief, then it is just as harmful to the individual as other avoidance dependencies. Healing comes from the whisper of your inner knowledge. The recovery process provides an opportunity for you to touch base with your core beliefs and values. Often, misbeliefs are replaced with truths about yourself, your family, and others. You can do this. You discover who is there for you, accepting everything about you unconditionally. Reclaiming your emotions and expressing your feelings make way for lasting healthy relationships.

"If you weep because the sun has set, your own tears will never let you see the stars" (Hindu proverb).

Recovery does *not* mean that you forget the person. The love is left with you. That love initially feels like a wound, and as you progress in your healing, the scar remains. That scar may bother you from time to time, but it does not interfere with your ability to live the healthy, productive life that you were meant to live. Some participants have expressed that they appreciate all the scars that life has given them as a testament to having loved and been loved.

"The deeper that sorrow carves into your being, the more joy you can contain" (Kahlil Gibran).

On a personal level, I know that as sad as it was to watch my sister die and leave such a young family, I know that it was her who became my inspiration to talk about loss and grief. Each seminar I give and each group I facilitate, she is with me. I tell my students and my groups about her. It feels good to be making something good come out of her death.

Recently, I was asked which death was more difficult for me: my mother's or my sister's death. It dawned on me that I may have answered that question with a different response over the last few decades. I was young at age nineteen when my mother died, and I distinctly recall thinking that she had at least lived most of her life, having married and had a family. It was only when I approached the age of forty that I realized how short her forty-seven years really were. Another influencing factor was that I was in nursing school and was the main contact between her surgeon and the family. As a nursing student, I was expected to shoulder that responsibility, and that was empowering. Withholding the information of her terminal illness from both my parents in 1969 was acceptable medical practice. I was living in nurses' residence, and my colleagues provided a strong support. The hospital was small. All staff was aware of my loss, and empathy abounded. My mother died twelve days before I wrote my RN exams. Graduation was a highlight clouded by the reality of what my family was facing at home.

One busy baking afternoon, I decided to make my mom's tomato soup cake. As I opened the oven to remove the cake, I felt as though I was transported to another time with my mother standing next to me in the kitchen. I could feel her presence with a keen sense of knowing she was there. My husband entered the kitchen and quietly asked, "Are you OK?" He said that I was pale and unusually still.

I cherish that moment. Some research identifies such experiences as olfactory hallucinations. I prefer to call them sweet visits from loved ones. That happened to me twenty-one years after my mother's death. I have made that recipe (attached) on numerous occasions since.

My sister's death was difficult because she was too young. She was leaving a two-year-old son and a young husband. Yet it was easier for reasons already explained. My relationship with her and our ability to connect honestly made it easier for me to accept her death.

I received many cards of sympathy after my sister, Alice, died. One in particular made sense to me. I transferred the verse to a plaque that I could display in my home. I often copied the verse when it became my turn to send words of sympathy. I also posted it outside the chapel door at my place of work.

The verse reads below:

> We are all God's children
> From our morning hour of birth
> He lets us Live, Laugh and Love
> And have our Day on Earth
> He guards us through the Afternoon
> 'Til Sunset's rays are cast
> Then One by One, with Gentle Words
> He calls us Home at Last.

Decades later when that friend's husband died, I sent her the verse and explained to her how much it had meant to me throughout the years. She was surprised and appreciative of the full circle.

Another kind gesture after Alice's funeral was the gift of a small African violet. I kept it for years until my overrated gardening skills failed. Forty-one years later, the African violet remains one of my favorite plants. Upon my retirement, I received a second African violet as a gift from a long-time friend who would have no idea of my appreciation for the plant. My heart was touched by his kind gesture and in sweet memory of my sister.

Alice had made her plans and her peace, and she was ready to give up the suffering. She knew she was going to a better place and that we would meet again. I knew her son would be well taken care of based on Alice's choice of caregiver. The first time I realized her son had an amazing voice was at a school concert years later when he was a preteen. He sang "Tears in Heaven" by Eric Clapton.

Recently, I found myself seated next to an old colleague at a concert. We started chatting. When Alice's son received a standing ovation after his voice and piano-playing performance wowed the audience, I bragged that he was my nephew. She shared that she had worked with Alice and never knew what had happened to her young son after her death. She leaned over and whispered, "Imagine if Alice could see him now." I chose to believe she does.

Everyone Grieves Differently

I consider myself an instrumental griever. Whenever I grieve, I am motivated to do something. I am not one to cry easily unless I am frustrated by my anger. The intuitive griever is one who typically expresses grief emotionally through tears and is generally assigned to women. I am reminded of my childhood when the girl next door died. Her mother was crying in the kitchen for a long time, while her father busied himself outdoors, tending to physically tiring chores.

Following my husband's death, I was approached by several and heard whispers from others that eventually, I "would have to cry." I remember being in church for my mother's funeral, watching all the nurses in caps and capes filling some pews and thinking how beautiful they all looked. My sixteen-year-old brother pushed Mom's casket to the front of the church, and I was impressed by how strong he looked, white-gloved hands firmly on the casket. The church was full. Tears were plentiful. I did not cry.

A dissonant griever is one who tries to exemplify what expected grieving looks like according to onlookers. Most persons are stronger in intuitive or instrumental ways of grieving. Your way of grieving is the right way. Don't be a dissonant griever.

Candy Lightner was undoubtedly devastated when her thirteen-year-old Cari was killed by a drunk driver. She founded Mothers Against Drunk Drivers (MADD) in 1980 to stop drunk drivers and to offer support for victim families. Today, there is at least one MADD office in every Canadian province and in every US state.

Closer to home, Gilles Boudreau and Friends Cancer Help Fund was established by his wife, Melina, following Gilles's terminal battle with cancer. She would tell you that during her husband's illness, he and his family received so much support from the community (VON, hospital staff, doctors, pharmacists, family, and people they did not even know). After his passing, his family could not think of a better way to keep his memory alive than by helping those in the community on their cancer journey. The closest Regional Cancer Centre is in Halifax, Nova Scotia, over three hundred kilometers from Yarmouth, Nova Scotia. Since 2013, this charity has raised annual revenues averaging $40,000. All has been raised through privately arranged fund-raising activities and charitable donations. As of 2018, this fund has provided financial assistance from ninety to one hundred Yarmouth County residents traveling for cancer care.

I recall a kind gesture extended to Gilles's widow during her grief journey. A thoughtful friend created pillows by stuffing some of Gilles's shirts, leaving the arms of the shirts attached to provide snuggly hugs. Melina has since created a lovely quilt with material from her husband's shirts. Love is a wonderful thing.

Around the support group circle, many items created in memory have brought comfort to grievers. One business wrote a poem about the deceased that they displayed in the workplace. Another brought a funny-faced cat ornament that she said was given to her in memory of the humor her husband always shared with others. It became her one thing to smile at on a daily basis. One fifteen-year-old participant brought a bottle of peanuts to the group—her grandfather's favorite.

Sharing these mementos was another way to further encourage conversations about the deceased. Talk eases some of the pain.

LOOKING FOR ANSWERS

After Alice died, I was struggling to find a reason for her early death. Alice and I had both been young wives and mothers beginning a new profession that we loved. We were focused on youth and social engagements with family and friends. Almost as a child becoming aware of mortality, I began to ponder suffering. Her suffering was over, but what about the loved ones left behind? What about their suffering? I found myself looking beyond my personal loss and wondering about suffering in general.

Suffering is not limited to the death of a loved one. Many of you can attest to that. Some of you have suffered things that nobody else knows, some too painful to recall, let alone share. Some of the suffering is not visible. It can include the loss of a dream, the pain of being lonely, or the pain of being deceived or totally ignored. Nobody is immune to suffering. For those who choose the pain, moments of greatest growth can be learned when we are suffering.

Is it when we give of ourselves that we find the sweetest joy? Many have attested that money and fame do not bring happiness on their own, but it is in service and support of others that we feel at our best.

LOSING A LOVED ONE TO DEMENTIA

My work journey with persons suffering from Alzheimer's and related dementias has taught me that some journeys are more difficult than loss associated with death. One loving wife shared this after her spouse died years after struggling with Alzheimer's disease: "I lost him twice. First when he forgot who I was, and finally, I lost him to death." She tearfully told of the years she had watched him helplessly as he slowly deteriorated.

As in most sad journeys, we do thankfully find nuggets of joy. My dad at age one hundred was a testament to perseverance in the midst of grief. As a daughter, I was privileged to share some of his experience firsthand.

Dad's roots can be traced back to France in the 1600s. The family name was recorded in the twelfth century and disappeared in France after the eighteenth century as the families only had girls. Dad's namesake was the first of my ancestors to travel to America, specifically Port Royal, Nova Scotia, with his young wife in 1662. They raised a large family, and their children married French girls who continued the lineage. During the 1755 expulsion of the Acadians, families scattered throughout Nova Scotia and the United States. Dad's great-grandfather was born locally in Cape Sable Island, and his grandfather was born in the village of my birth, Sluice Point, on the southwestern point of Nova Scotia.

Dad was born a twin on March 28, 1918, the third pregnancy of his mother's ten gestations. His twin and two siblings died of early infant illnesses. When Dad was age seven, Dad's father drowned, leaving behind his widow with a ten-month-old baby and a house full of children. An aunt took the baby to live with her in the United States. Dad was age eleven when his mother died of pneumonia. She was laid in her casket in the living room of the family home. During the wake, there was an earth tremor that shook the dishes in the cupboard and on the table. An aunt reassured the children that it was nothing, to not be afraid, and that it would pass. No tremor has been felt in that home to this day, eighty-nine years later. Tante Annie, who had brought up my grandmother, arranged for the children to be placed. As customary in those rural areas, orphans were cared for by relatives. Some siblings moved as far away as Massachusetts. Dad was "adopted" by an older couple down the road. The husband, named Roubinne, was an uncle to dad's mother. He had been born on an isolated piece of land and had married a kind lady from across the river. They cared for a mentally challenged son and an orphaned seven-year-old grandson when Dad moved in. When Dad was fourteen, his family was again facing death. N'oncle Roubinne, as Dad called him, died of coronary disease, leaving his widow to care for the home, two children, and a mentally challenged adult son. I never knew the woman who brought up my dad, but I know from the stories he told that Tante Deline was a woman of faith, of kindness, and of love. I grew up with many stories about her, and in Dad's older age, his memory often returned to those days when his character had been strengthened through her example despite adversity. Johnny, her handicapped son, lived to age fifty. Her grandson died of tuberculosis at age twenty-one. Tante Deline died at her home at age ninety-two.

By the time Dad married my mom on June 3, 1940, he was no stranger to loss and grief. He inherited the old and vacated family house by paying the back taxes owed on it. Gradually, they repaired the home and raised nine children, including a severely mentally handicapped offspring. In the early years of their marriage, they were contacted by the local priest to look after his recently widowed eighty-two-year-old aunt. Her only child had died at birth, and she could not manage by herself. Dad and his brother drove to her home to get her. She had never sat in a car before. She perched herself on the upright part of the car seat with her feet on the seat and her head scrunched against the roof of the car; my uncle was snickering in the back seat. Mom gave her the bedroom next to the living room. She lived with us for two years. My memory of her is Mom telling us children not to get too close to her as she might hit us with her cane.

My childhood memories of my dad are of a hard-working man who earned a living by working at several moneymaking opportunities. These included harvesting and drying peat moss on the gravel between the dirt road and our property, traveling over one hundred miles to purchase apples to sell door-to-door, being a car salesman, maintaining a vegetable garden ploughed with a hand tiller attached to the horse, keeping a cow and a pig, and meeting the train six days a week to deliver the mail to six villages. I recall him saying this of his own childhood: "We were lucky. We always had something to eat." Dad seemed content to accept what life handed him and maintained a sense of humor despite life's challenges. He was not demonstrative in his affection, yet I felt loved and safe in his presence.

Growing up, Dad was the disciplinarian who would stand at the bottom of the stairs and threaten to come upstairs if we didn't settle down for sleep. I pictured the kindling he had in his hand, borrowed from the pile that was ready to start the morning fire. The house was always cozy and warm when we came down for breakfast. I don't recall him ever climbing those stairs. Mom would often promise consequences to our misbehaviors "as soon as Dad gets home." He was also the guy who drove us kids to the gas station / country store in a nearby village on nice Sunday afternoons. The back of the pickup truck was full of us kids, while he and Mom sat in the front with my mentally handicapped sister. I hold vivid memories of him coming out of that store, approaching the truck with upheld hands holding multiple dripping vanilla ice cream cones.

He was also the guy who met my date at the door one night after he considered it a long time span between the movie and the drive home. "If you want to date a loose woman, there are some in the next village!" he yelled. I married that date in what was called a shotgun wedding in those days. Eleven years and two sons later, when I went home to tell Dad I was getting divorced, he said, "What you do with your life is your business."

After twenty-nine years of marriage, my mom died in 1969 after a six-month illness. I never saw Dad cry, although I heard his anger. Following the death of my second husband in 1999, I visited Dad and his words were simple yet comforting: "I bet you thought I was an old man when your mother died." I felt as though he understood. He had been there. Throughout my life, my parents seemed to accept death and hardships as a natural part of life. I often heard Dad say, "Sometimes, God thinks it's time for him to come and take a person up to heaven where there is no suffering." He also quipped, "Everybody wants to go to heaven, but nobody wants to die." I have no doubt that the faith Tante Deline passed on to my dad carried him throughout all his times of disappointments and loss. He was also leading by example, if not by words.

Dad remarried while my youngest sibling was still at home. His new wife was the widow of a man who had been brought up with my mom. We had known the family as kids when they would occasionally visit our home on Sunday afternoons. My memory brings me back to those times we would hide behind the front room sofa so we could stare at her thick glasses. Giggles often followed.

Both our lives were busy after his second marriage, and visits became irregular although always pleasant. I was pleased to see Dad resettled with a new relationship and new activities. In those days, I wondered why they frequently visited the funeral home and attended services for persons they barely knew. They both understood the generosity of supporting persons who were grieving. Years later, I understood that also.

Dad's journey into dementia began long before he showed signs of cognitive impairment. His wife became dependent on him as she struggled with obsessive behaviors and memory loss. He moved into the caregiver role without complaint despite losing sleep while her sleep patterns changed. They hired Jean, a neighbor, who provided housekeeping services and became their companion and friend. They both required home care assistance, especially with bathing, a chore family could not provide.

Continuing Care, a government agency providing home care, was contacted. Dad was hesitant at first and complained that some workers appeared too young to be doing that kind of work. An older woman was assigned to them, much to his relief. Regrettably, as per department policy on seniority, that staff was reassigned. My objections to the department based on client comfort and preference fell on deaf ears.

One fall, from which he could not get up, sent Dad to the emergency department at the local hospital. He was exhausted and frail. His wife was admitted to a nursing home in February 2013, the same home where her sister had lived and died. My father had accompanied his wife on many of those visits. Dad was admitted to the hospital's chronic care unit. He developed pneumonia, and we feared his physical health would deteriorate. He was having longer periods of confusion. On his better days, he would speak his mind with unfiltered opinions mixed with expressions of humor. He was coping better than I was. Admission to a busy hospital unit creates multiple changes in routine—some of which seem to be policy based rather than person centered. Although the majority of the staff were pleasant, some lacked training in the field of geriatrics. Change in environment, fast-paced change in personnel attending to his care, and change in his ability to communicate compounded his confusion. The policy to add sedation to a misdiagnosed reaction to change and loss frustrated me. Dad managed to find some positive adaptations through it all.

Although changes in brain tissue indicating dementia were first identified by Dr. Alois Alzheimer in 1906, there still exists a general lack of understanding about the illness. No mention of dementia was covered in my nursing education program in the late 1960s. I recall some physicians referring to senility as a normal part of aging. It is not. Growing up in the 1950s, I watched a village provide supervisory care to an old gentleman who would often wander off away from his home. He would enter into various homes through unlocked doors, as was common in those days, and sit and mumble or pick up an article and fuss over it until he felt it was time to move on. One clever old lady next door would give him yarn to unravel, occupying him for hours as she conversed with him in soft affirmative words in her quiet country kitchen.

The Alzheimer Society of Nova Scotia has invested time and resources in researching, informing, and supporting persons with Alzheimer's and related dementia. I was continuously surprised at the number of families who admitted loved ones to the nursing home who remained unaware of the physiology of the disease, misunderstanding symptoms as controllable behaviors. I did not expect to observe this lack of knowledge among hospital personnel. Regrettably, I did.

There are approximately seventy types of dementia. Although symptoms are more prevalent in the population over the age of sixty-five, dementia is *not* a normal part of aging. The Alzheimer Society of Nova Scotia estimates one out of eleven Canadian persons with dementia. That statistic translates to 15,000 residents of Nova Scotia with an increasing aging demographic.

Dementias present as a gradual decline in cognitive function. Overall brain function is affected and can be related to vascular insufficiency or specific frontotemporal diseases such as Lewy body, which forms abnormal structures that destroy neurons or affect neuron function. Lewy body disease generally has a rapid progression until fatal.

Other types of dementias can cause a roller coaster of symptoms lasting for years. Good days alternating with bad days are often misinterpreted as willful and intentional behaviors. I have heard numerous comments relating to observers' common conclusions: "I know they are just behaving badly when I am around" or "They know better than that" or "That behavior is just for show." In reality, nothing could be further from the truth. I like the clever statement that was initially coined regarding children but applies so well to persons suffering with dementia: "They are not giving you a hard time. They are having a hard time."

Other dementias are reversible, such as cognitive impairments caused by sedatives or antidepressants. Adding these prescriptions to an elderly person who is experiencing major life changes—such as loss of health, loss of independence plus hospitalization—is now being recognized as a polypharmacy issue that needs to be addressed. Medications are not always the best approach despite proven successes in the treatment of multiple diseases. The majority of medication research studies are based on middle-aged control groups and not on elderly persons. Pediatric medications are adjusted to age-related dosages, while many geriatric dosages are not adjusted despite knowledge that detoxifying organs, such as the liver and kidneys, may have slower functions in older age.

Urinary tract infections, pneumonia, constipation, anemia, and dehydration are other causes of reversible dementias. One elderly lady was admitted to the nursing home where I was fortunate enough to work all those years. Her admission diagnosis was Alzheimer's disease after months of mental decline. After her thyroid medication was adjusted, she regained her cognitive health and became an influential part of the social fabric that made the home a great place to live.

Delirium presents as an acute disturbed state of mind often seen with high fever or other disorders. My first recollection of delirium was as a young child observing the local drunks who staggered past my house after frequenting the bootlegger down the road. Eighty-five percent of palliative care persons will experience some delirium at the end of life. Encouraging loved ones to have any conversation while the person remains lucid is an important step in sharing that final goodbye.

Alzheimer's disease warrants a lot of attention as it is the largest component of all dementias, recorded as over 64 percent and affecting more females than males. My most memorable patient with the disease was a male in his forties who no longer recognized his wife or his children.

The diagnosis of Alzheimer's disease is confirmed by examination of the brain cells following death. Most recent ultrasounds of the brain have assisted in the diagnosis as the appearance of shrinking brain cells is evident. Plaques that I imagine to be sticky gum attach themselves to brain cells and form thread-like tangles that progressively erode the brain. The disease remains irreversible as research continues.

My knowledge was at times a hindrance as I watched his journey throughout his hospitalization and tried to be polite while suggesting Dad's care meet a reasonable standard. Advocacy for a loved one requires patience. On some days, that patience was missing. Looking back, it was probably best that the three meetings I requested with management were never acknowledged. Perhaps they were too busy.

Dad had always stated that he and his wife would never go into a nursing home. His plan was to move to Annapolis Valley, where he had bought apples for years. He often mentioned that the weather and the orchards were appealing and the people were very nice there.

The day arrived when we had to transfer Dad from the hospital to the same nursing home his wife now resided in. My older brother assisted him to stand and to pivot into the front seat of my car. Dad said, "That was easy with the help of a giant. Now how are you going to get me out of here? With a can opener?" He was pleased to be getting out of the hospital and going for a drive. He asked where we were going, and I hesitantly told him the truth, "We are going to Villa Saint Joseph." He paused ever so briefly to say, "Are they looking for a bishop? Good enough, I'm applying for the job." Along the drive, I slowed the car to let ducks cross the road, and he was happy to watch them. I was impressed at how sharp his vision was. As I pulled into the long driveway, he said, "Wow, a moneyman must live here." His dementia felt like a blessing.

A moneyman was what Dad called anyone who had wealth. An outsider was generally an English-speaking individual. In 1970, he had told me of an outsider who had come into the village to place a For Sale sign on a piece of land. That outsider was a person from the local town who had lived there for forty years. Dad held a high respect for outsiders and any person in authority. The only exception was if he knew they voted for Conservatives. Persons who drove anything but a Dodge were of questionable decision-making abilities as well.

That first night when my youngest brother and I left him at the table, he wondered why we were not joining him for supper. Then he asked who was going to take care of him that night. I told him that the nurses would. With a brave face, he leaned upward to kiss my face. With heavy hearts, we walked away.

His adjustment to the home was nothing short of amazing. Having worked in a nursing home for twenty-seven years, I was all too familiar with difficult transitions and guilt-ridden family members. His reconnection with his wife was sweet to witness as they would often sit holding hands. The leaning from his wheelchair to hers for a kiss was not always accomplished but often attempted. The staff exceeded my expectations. Dad did not seem to notice that he was in a wheelchair, often referring to it as his car. If he did, he never mentioned it to me. He referred to the restraint across his lap as his seatbelt.

Each visit brought new stories. I asked him if he would like to go outside for some fresh air. His reply was quick, "I was strolling down Main Street yesterday, and I noticed a guy eyeing up my mustache. Next thing I knew, he was following me with a pair of scissors so he could steal it. I'm staying in today, keeping my mustache safe!"

Dad started telling me that it was a good thing he was where he was because some people would be lonesome without him. He bonded with an elderly gentleman from our village, telling me that Bernard needed a friend as he was a widower.

Adjusting to a nursing home generally takes several weeks to several months. He seemed to adjust to his new surroundings faster than most. I was anticipating a change in the acceptance he presented.

He seemed to always have a story to tell on my visits. Some were embellished, while some were a version of the world according to Dad: "I played poker last night. Won five bucks!" or "I'm spit-shining clean. They washed me in a gunboat (his version of the full-size elevated ultrasonic bathtub)."

The main lounge provided him a view of the front entrance, and he would recognize persons approaching the doorway. He welcomed all persons he knew as if they were coming in to visit him. He and his wife spent a fair amount of time watching TV on a big screen that he believed he recently purchased. Always wanting to entertain, he would sometimes pretend to bite his wife whenever she leaned in for a kiss.

I told Dad I was going to Rome. "You wouldn't catch me flying that far. No wonder planes crash. They run out of gas!" Upon my return, he said, "You were gone a long time. Did the pope ask about me?"

Amid those conversations, he often returned to the chores he needed to do around the house. "Today, I went to Carl's store for a few groceries. I noticed that they were removing soil off my land to build the new bridge. Good for me. They are paying me a hefty price for it!"

That same day, he looked over from his wheelchair to another resident sitting in his wheelchair and said, "If I ever get like that, *une balle* (a bullet)." In his mind, he was well, and for that I was grateful.

Often, he would look at his wife sitting beside him and say, "A chi t'est le p'tit ga?" (Whose little boy are you?)—a comment he had made to his daughters and granddaughters throughout the years.

As loving as they were, they had their spats. As his wife became weaker, the staff would escort her out of the lounge before him for an earlier bedtime. At different times, both began conversations about the other seeing someone else. Their routine of going to bed together for decades was unraveling. Dad's suspicions escalated during one of my visits as they shared verbal accusations. Twenty minutes later, the entire conversation was forgotten. Memory loss sometimes has some advantages.

The hallway to his wife's room necessitated wheeling his chair past a breezy ventilation vent. He would often comment that "a fella should have a boat and oars to travel through here."

He was confined to his room at one point due to a contagious influenza, and I expected to see a sick man on that visit. Dressed in an institutional gown and sweater, he was sitting by the window as I entered his room. His greeting was enthusiastic with a big smile and an eagerness to show me the expansion he was adding to his house. His view was of the new nursing home addition being built. Several men were shingling the roof, all of them wearing hard hats and safety harnesses. He pointed out that although you had to tie the workers so they would stay on the roof to finish the job, they were damn good workers once you got them up there.

His observation skills and sharp wit opened my eyes to his surroundings as I watched him accept his new normal. As elderly persons shuffled past his door bent over walkers, he would politely greet them. He would sometimes wait until they were out of earshot and grin and comment with "And me without my slingshot" or "That tall one doesn't need a ladder to go peeping in windows."

Often, I would hear him say, "They are all nice here" as he won their hearts with his humor. Some staff told me he was teaching them French words.

He loved to sing out loud, especially Charlie Pride's "Crystal Chandelier," his favorite for years. One time, he was rendering a loud version of the verse, and a visitor approached him, looked at his wife, and jokingly asked her if she wanted to dance. Dad interrupted his chorus with "Hey, you want to fight?"

There was an elderly gentleman sitting next to Dad in the lounge. He was not roused by any conversation or loud noise. Suddenly, the man coughed, and Dad pretended to be totally surprised, commenting, "Get the shovel!" (In Dad's day, graves were dug by hand—one man with a shovel.)

His wife complained of her forgetfulness. "Quit drinking," he quipped, "and your memory will improve!" She was becoming more particular about her blanket covering her from her feet to her neck even while sitting in her wheelchair. One hot summer afternoon, after repeated attempts to meet her demands, he looked at me and said, "We are expecting a snowstorm."

He made leaving him easy with a smiling face and usual words: "Come again. We will be right here, and I'm going to leave the door unlocked."

He had good stories. He would talk about killing the pig and making blood pudding. He explained that the French word *Mashqui* referred to the gum retrieved from under a tree bark and used to seal roof shingles and prevent rainwater leaks. He had his own great ideas. "You would think with the price of gas someone would have invented a pill to make your feet go faster." He talked about contacting a municipal councillor to secure funding for a snow fence to be erected by a portion of road often hampered by heavy snowfalls. He had not driven by that open marsh for years.

Some days, the staff would carefully groom his wife and wheel her to the lounge to sit beside my dad for short periods of time. On such a day, I came in to visit, and he said, "I am sitting with her even though she is not aware that I am here." He expressed concern over her weight loss, pointing to her emaciated arms, adding that she rarely opens her eyes. I approached her and kissed her cheek. She opened her eyes, looked at me, and said, "*T'est belle.*" (You are pretty.) Dad quipped, "She is further gone than I thought. *A perd la vue!*" (Her eyesight is going.)

As his wife's health deteriorated, she became more demanding of his attention while they were together. Her anxiety was often not calmed by his numerous attempts to console her, and one could sense his helplessness. At times, he would say, "Let's visit the sick little girl." During these times, I felt he was reliving a time when Alice was sick. He would use all his energy to get up from his wheelchair, hanging on to his wife's bedrail, give her a kiss, and tell her to get some rest.

When Dad turned ninety-five, he proudly announced that he was ninety-six. When he turned ninety-seven, he said that he couldn't possibly be that old, adding that the priest must have lied on his baptismal certificate.

Despite his decline in physical health, he chose to accept his new surroundings. He would often talk about what needed to be done around the house, such as painting the south side or adding an expansion to the porch. He frequently asked if there was enough food in the fridge or pantry and if he needed to go to the store. A patient listening ear and an assurance that we would look after those chores in the near future always seemed to ease his mind. Redirecting him to the present environment was easily accepted, and to this day, I remain thankful for that. Those times of him feeling the need to revisit his lifelong responsibilities quickly turned into humor. He seemed to have developed chronic chest congestion, and he would often follow a bout of coughing with a comment, such as, "This cough is going to shorten my life to 105 years."

As Fathers' Day was approaching, I asked him what he would like as a gift. He answered, "Not a truck as they are too high to climb aboard! How about a chocolate bar?"

During his moments of clarity, I took the advantage of asking him how he felt about his new surroundings. I asked, "Do you like it here?" He replied, "I do because they are all so nice. They even comb my hair! But I wish they didn't wake me up so early. It's not like I'm going to pick up Danny to go cutting wood for the day." It was an activity he often did and loved. He added that he liked being in the same place where he can visit his wife and that he liked that they take good care of her. He was happy that they were adding new construction to the home. "The government has the money. They owe us that building for every dime they took from every dollar we earned over the years."

Bringing him news of the world outside the villa always interested him. He was pleased when I told him my brother and his wife were on vacation in Mexico. "Mexico! Good enough! Earl never stops working, handling two jobs! You know how much he likes to talk. We won't be able to get a word in edgewise when they come back. I wonder if he will still be able to speak English."

When I told him my sister Marilyn had a new job, he said, "Good. I didn't want to ask. Imagine if I asked and she said no. That wouldn't be good."

My brother and I were visiting one day when I told him I had just returned home from Cape Breton. He looked at me then at my brother. "Not in that Ford I hope. Now if somebody was to come in here to tell me one of my kids went crazy, I would say, 'I know which one. It's Bertha, still driving a Ford.'"

As his memory continued to diminish, he admitted that he was forgetful, and I volunteered that I was forgetful at times as well. He reassured me by pointing out that it's difficult to remember stuff as everything in the world is changing so fast. I could feel that he was alert as he shared, "Not like back when we were living in Sluice Point. Look at all the stuff we worried about . . . for nothing! We are still here, and all is well."

We reminisced about his life, having married twice to two wonderful women. I cautiously asked, "Do you think about Mom?" A tear ran down his cheek, "Of course I do. Do you think I could ever forget?" And for the first time since my mom died in 1969, he was not silent on her cancer and our loss. He offered, "She didn't want to talk about it, you know. We knew, but we didn't say too much. I would tell her that a lot of people had it, and they got better."

I moved on to them raising nine children. In Dad fashion, a twinkle in his eye showed up as if to cheer me. He laughed and quickly replied, "I'm glad no more kids came knocking on my door." And then he suggested that I better go home before it gets dark as I needed to go to bed.

He liked to attend mass. The life-size statues of Saint Joseph and the Holy Mother behind the altar brought him a familiarity he had experienced throughout his lifetime. He also expressed that it would be nice if some sermons could come up with a new story as he had heard a lot of them over and over again. "I mean, how many times do we need to hear that the bad son ran away, spent all his father's money, and then was welcomed back?" His tales included one of a prayer so long it extended to *les Damasse* (a woodlot he owned deep into the forest). One particular day, when the nun offered him the Eucharist, he said, "Why not! I plan on staying Catholic for at least one more year." There were times that his humor could have annoyed Sister; however, she understood and fully accepted him even when he extended his tongue, received the Eucharist, and yelled, "Down the hatch!" while smacking his lips.

On one visit, I found him sitting in his usual place beside his wife in the main lounge. I noticed he was shivering. I asked the RN to check his temperature, and he did have a fever. He would not have complained, but he admitted he felt a whole lot better in bed. The nurse placed the blood pressure monitor on his arm, and he said, "It's not my age that is making me sick. I'm only ninety-five." On that day, he let me feed him. I have fed many persons throughout my career, but I had never fed my dad.

A few days later, he was back in the lounge. "Nothing new today except New York!" he yelled as I walked in. His wife volunteered that they had attended mass this morning, adding that God is everywhere. Dad says, "I heard he was playing guitar at the club in Surette's Island last night!" His eyes lit up, and then he got serious, reciting a French Bible verse and explaining that it means "People should never be afraid because God is with us always."

His wife asked for an apple, and I asked her if I should peel it. She paused, looked at me, and then all her teeth appeared through her widening smile. "It has been a long time since I had skin."

She made no secret of the intimacy they shared throughout their marriage. Dad's first hospitalization was at the age of eighty-four, when he suffered a heart attack. On his return home, his wife shared that she was careful not to lie too close to him in bed as she didn't want to get him too excited . . . until his heart got stronger. I answered, "You feel like it's been a long time?" She looked at Dad, smiled, and said, "You're telling me!" He dropped his head to the side, rolled his eyes back in the sockets, and stuck his tongue out to the side of his mouth." They both laughed out loud. "No, we are OK," he said. He quietly motioned to a younger resident sitting on the sofa, saying, "She's blind."

What was heartwarming about those days was that they were both generally content. Despite their disorientation, they seemed to find a common understanding. I arrived one day, and they both told me the story that they had just been making their bed together. "She lets me help, but she's fussy." He smiled. I had witnessed that practice when they lived at home. I had tried to help her make the bed one time. She wanted to do it herself, aligning each pattern on the quilt with the bedsheets and pillowcases. As her dementia progressed at home, her behavior changed to a heightened obsessiveness with her household tasks. She developed the need to double-check the water taps to make sure they were not dripping and to check the door to ensure it was locked. Often, she would ask Dad to do repeat these assurances for her.

Research shows that some forms of cognitive impairment can lead to repetitive activity. One of my colleagues often warned us that the behaviors we obsess about during our adult life are bound to escalate with advancing age and become compulsive with dementia. We joked about this idea as a staff, making sure that we focused on fun. We decided housework should get less attention.

His wife was demonstrative in her affection, often holding his hand and saying, "He is a tease, but I love him." His response was invariably a grin, a squeal, and a spasmodic shaking of both arms. Often, they would share a midafternoon snack in the lounge. I brought them a buttered biscuit, some cheese, and hot tea with milk and sugar. Dad decided he was not hungry but visibly enjoyed watching his wife eating and licking her fingers. She reached for his untouched cheese and asked him if he was sure he didn't want it. "Nooooo, you go ahead. Do I look like a mouse?" After a few minutes of methodically wiping her lips, he said to her, "If you are trying to remove your lips, perhaps we can call dentist LeBlanc to assist you?" She loved men and often voiced her admiration. On one visit, my current husband leaned down to her wheelchair level to shake her hand. Before he could say hello, she smiled and said, "You're handsome."

Often, Dad would chat about my brother Roderick, his seventy-year-old son who died in his sleep. Roderick would be sitting in the rocking chair by their kitchen stove on most evenings for his usual visit. Dad understood about cremation but would often say that it was hard to imagine his son had died as it was as if he disappeared. "Sometimes, I think he is still here. I wish he was." His wife reached over to pat his arm and said, "He is in heaven. It's very nice there."

For the longest time, Dad maintained that his wife would get stronger and get better. "She needs to eat!" he would say. Throughout my career, I have heard many family members encouraging and some being adamant in getting sick loved ones to eat. I attended a palliative care conference at Baycrest Health Science Centre in Toronto and listened to a speaker who had miraculously recovered from a serious illness. She spoke of one of her hardships: being forced to eat when she had no appetite. She explained it this way: "Think about being nauseated and weak and people continuously poking at you to try and make you eat." Her words resonated with me.

Dad's wife became sicker and was no longer sitting with him in the lounge. I entered one day, and he yelled, "Bertha, I have something to ask you!" I felt that he was cognitively alert on this visit as he rarely called me by name. He asked if Alice was going to get better. Feeling that he meant his wife and not his daughter, I replied, "I could tell you a story that you may want to hear, but no, Dad, I don't believe she will get better." He pondered my answer then spoke, "The age is there, you know, and I don't believe she knows me anymore." With his usual approach to life's disappointments, he quickly shifted the conversation. Or was it dementia that delivered him from his present reality? He described being outside today, mowing the lawn on the ride-on tractor while a helper was riding another. "I only bought one ride-on, and I have no idea where the second one came from." He was disappointed that one son had sold the ox and the other son sold the horse. "How do they expect to make money after that cash is gone?" He described how he had to sneak up to the peak of the house to finish painting as his daughter Ella gets annoyed whenever he climbs a ladder.

On another day, he was visibly upset as soon as I entered the lounge. I feared his wife's condition may have worsened. He had a different concern. It was the new relationship that he wanted to discuss, the two elderly persons sitting on the couch, holding hands. The lady had dark hair, convincing Dad she was much too young for the likes of him! He explained that when he was widowed, he did not go looking for a girlfriend because "Who needs that bullshit!" I paused and answered, "It seems to me that I remember some women coming to ask you to go out with them." His eyes lit up, and he answered, "I tell you the problem. I was told just one drink. Who knew it was going to be a ten-ounce glass? Well, down the hatch it went. I *may* have found a girlfriend or two." As we were both enjoying reminiscing, the couple stood up and kissed, leaving the lounge hand in hand. Raising his voice loud enough to be heard by everyone, he said, "And there they go! Headed to the haymow no doubt!"

Dad decided to adapt. When he was first admitted, the facility expansion was being built, and large windows of the aging structure were susceptible to the heavy sounds of wind and pounding rain. I visited one morning after a particularly nasty storm he called a nor'easter. Dad greeted me with "This place was given to me. It's a good tight house. No wind will ever bother anyone here."

Dad held on to his view of loss. "You can't complain about life. As Tante Deline used to say, 'Expect a branch to stick out now and then.' She got on her knees every single day, and she left things up to God. I tried that, but my knees got too flat."

As his wife approached her palliative stage, he spent more time sitting with the other residents in the lounge. My husband and I were chatting with him one afternoon when he suggested we all go visit "the sick little girl" as he most recently referred to as his wife. We wheeled him to her room. She looked frail and unresponsive in her single bed covered by a pale institutional bedspread. He mustered all the strength he had unbuckling his seatbelt so he could stand on his own, while we stood guard to catch him if the need arose. He spoke these words to her, calling her by name, "It's Antoine. It's OK. You won't be sick much longer. Go to sleep." He kissed her forehead, and upon returning to the lounge with wet eyes, he said, "If you fellas have not had lunch, it's OK with me if you want to go now." It was in the middle of the afternoon, but I realized that on that day, he understood that death was near, and he wanted to grieve alone.

DYING

Dying is the difficult part of death. Dad's wife had a difficult last few months, making it harder for Dad to watch her struggle and not easy for us to witness the pain they both experienced. Having spent years as an obstetrical nurse, I see similarities in the transitions of birth and death. Some are easier than others, but the end result brings a mix of emotions that are a blessing to witness.

Having been fortunate to sit with numerous dying patients, I have witnessed many beautiful deaths. The first time I sat with a dying patient was daunting as I had limited knowledge of the dying process and knew less about the grief journey. The lessons that I gained from my dying patients enriched my comfort level that began with the honesty Alice shared with me during her journey.

It was the busy time of the shift at the nursing home where I worked when it became obvious that one elderly lady was entering the last stage of her life. You may know it as taking a turn for the worse. Her chronic illness was no longer manageable. I was scheduled to go off duty but chose to provide her with one-on-one care. She had shown her rough exterior on some occasions, critical of her care and family's and friends' infrequent visits. Her breathing became labored, and she expressed that she was concerned that God would not forgive her for the life she had lived. "I need to pray," she said, "but I'm too short of breath."

Somewhere in my memory files, I retrieved a story my mother had told me as a little child, and I shared it with her. "When we are too tired to pray, the angels come, and they take over." She believed. Her breathing calmed, and she told me of some of the ugly chapters in her life. I recalled reading that we all need to tell our truth to someone before we die. Her face relaxed, and she peacefully took her last breath.

I have witnessed several comatose and dying persons opening their eyes and extending their arm upward as if greeting a loving friend before taking that last breath. I have heard stories of anticipation from persons entering those last days of life. A good friend of mine who had experienced great financial success was diagnosed with a terminal illness. As he knew I was comfortable with the topic of death, we had numerous conversations about his expectations. He had no regrets at leaving this life earlier than most. He was appreciating the beauty in nature and the love of family and friends to a heightened level. I recall him saying, "Turn off the news. Talk to everyone you can." He knew that his death meant that he was going to perfect his piano playing in the next dimension.

At the core of grief is walking the dying journey with a loved one. Having an understanding of the dying process can provide loved ones some assistance during a time that is more than what you think you can handle.

During the last days of life, it is expected that the dying person will become focused on leaving this earth rather than staying connected to loved ones. In the palliative care world, there is an old understanding that dying persons will do three things before an anticipated death. They will seek to make amends, wish to say goodbye, and will turn inwardly to find their own peace. The last step is withdrawing to the self. Knowing this allows loved ones to be open to what the person wishes to say and to be accepting of difficult conversations. I wish I had listened to my mom's concerns while she was still coherent and willing to talk instead of comforting her with false assurances.

I have witnessed family members sobbing at a patient's bedside and begging them not to go. That is understandable; however, when we know better, we do better. The dying process will rob your loved one of energy and often causes restlessness and agitation. Your calm and gentle presence can soothe them, while your anxiety can be transferred to them. Quiet music of their liking, soft lighting, gentle touch, and a quiet space provide comfort. A full room of talkative visitors is not recommended.

Body Changes

Body changes include longer sleep periods, loss of appetite with difficulty swallowing, fluctuating body temperatures, and pallor of skin. A high temperature and perspiration are not unusual. Generally, mottling and a bluish discoloration of arms and legs become noticeable as death approaches. Nurses often note a grayish appearance of the nose as another sign that death is imminent. Many dying persons will have chest congestion, and some will have pain. Medications are always indicated to relieve these symptoms. On rare occasions, I have heard concerns from family members that they would like no medications so their loved ones can remain as alert as possible. Sometimes, staying alert means the pain will not be managed.

Encourage conversation before the last days of life. Listen to what they want to tell you. Sit down. Make eye contact and ask questions, such as "What are your thoughts about that?" or "I would like for you to tell me more." As difficult as the conversations may be, you will look back and be pleased you had them. It is not unusual for dying persons to tell you of their plans for the future as though they are not dying. It is OK to be accepting of where they want to be rather than correcting their statements. Sometimes, the dying person needs to say things out loud in order to make sense of their uncertain future. Never underestimate the beauty of saying nothing. Just be there, present and attentive.

Older persons never cease to amaze me. I shall give her a false name of Bernice. She rang her buzzer, asking to go to the hospital as her breathing was getting worse. I explained to her that I could send her; however, I did not feel they could offer her more than what they did on previous visits, which included a bumpy ambulance ride and a long wait on a stretcher in an overcrowded, brightly lit, noisy hallway only to be seen and returned to the nursing home on another prescription that she often refused to take. I reviewed her long medical history with her, and we talked about expecting this day, where nothing more could be offered. With a strong voice, she said, "Si je vais mourir, y faut priez Dieu." (If it's my time to die, we need to pray.) Another RN was at her bedside with me, and she asked one of us to pray *le Notre Pere* (the Our Father). Bernice spoke Acadian French all her life, so I asked my colleague to recite the prayer as I could only recall the prayer in English. My colleague admitted a reluctance to pray out loud.

The elderly roommate jumped out of her bed and approached Bernice's bedside telling us to move aside. She touched Bernice's face and arms and blurted out, "You're having the death sweats" and proceeded to pray *le Notre Pere*. Bernice immediately started naming persons she was going to soon meet in heaven. She recalled persons from the village who died years ago and some whom I had forgotten. She looked at me and said, "And I'm going to see your mother again." She took her last peaceful breath shortly thereafter. She had a beautiful death that we were blessed to witness.

I could tell you of many more, including the one who asked me to play a spiritual CD. Before closing her eyes, she said, "The music in heaven is much better."

Faith is a beautiful thing.

My Dad

Dad continued to show signs of cognitive deterioration mixed with moments of clarity. Two strangers walked past our seating in the lounge, and Dad extended his hand and introduced himself, "Hello, my name is Anthony, and this is my daughter Bertha. I was the mailman in Sluice Point for forty-six years." The gentlemen introduced themselves and said they were here to visit a friend. They asked Dad how long he had been at the villa. He replied, "This is my home. I was born here. So come visit any time!"

My dad always was impressed with vehicles, cars, and trucks. After my two sons visited and shared photos of some cars they had raced in, they were able to ignite some positive memory. The next day, I reminded him of their visit. "I didn't like it!" he said. "It was too short! Are they coming back for Christmas?" Within seconds, he moved to another of his realities and showed me the new shirt he was wearing that a (long-time deceased) friend had just purchased for him. He proudly displayed the new wedding band that he and a long-time neighbor and widow (also deceased) had recently bought together. In those days, he had full control of his vocabulary, and his eyesight provided him with stimulation. He'd say, "Look at that one's hairdo. She must have used a horsebrush to comb her hair." or "One came in this morning with face powder so thick I barely knew her. Lipstick up to her eyebrows."

When his wife died, his mind wandered between remembering and forgetting. Together, as a family, we decided that he should participate in the viewing at the funeral home. The staff had him dressed in his suit and tie when I arrived to pick him up. He looked well. He was sitting in his wheelchair, and he was pleased to be going out. I reminded him that we were going to the funeral home. "Let's go!" he said. It was a short distance by car, but after several minutes, he asked me why we were driving so far. I thought that perhaps he was thinking that his wife was still in her room down the corridor. Family members assisted him from the car to his wheelchair and moved him inside to greet the people gathered to pay their respects. We were all surprised at the appropriate greetings and responses he shared with everyone while being the perfect host in a funeral home setting. He recognized relatives that he had not seen in years and did not seem to tire from so much activity. On return to the nursing home, he shared enthusiasm at having visited with so many people. In the weeks following the funeral, he would sometimes ask to go see his wife. At times, I would tell the little white lie that can soften the reality of a confused mind and suggest that we wait until she was awake. At other times, I would have to remind him that she was in heaven. He readily accepted both responses. I frequently realized and was always thankful for his acceptance of whatever situation he faced.

In my work experience, I had frequently met persons with dementia who could not be calmed or redirected with words or medication. Many family members have to witness loved ones struggling with frustration, anxiety, and aggressiveness. Despite the development of programs such as gentle persuasive approaches to care and management of challenging behaviors, some persons with dementia still struggle and suffer through their journey. One factor that could improve quality of care is increased funding for caregivers and multidisciplinary support staff. It is a well-documented fact that staffing ratios are inadequate in long-term care institutions and home care settings. Despite these realities, I was always impressed at how well all nursing and support staff were able to manage my dad's care.

When Dad turned ninety-eight, it was not a huge surprise that he became more forgetful and often irritated by his confusion. He started showing signs of aggression when personal care had to be administered as he struggled to understand staff intentions. Hallucinations complicated his peaceful environment, and his sleep patterns became interrupted. With careful medication administration, he was able to relax and regain some cognitive abilities but not without causing difficulty for staff and a new reality for family members. This pattern would periodically reappear, although overall, he remained reasonably content.

When Dad turned ninety-nine, he could communicate fairly well although his world was shrinking to his immediate surroundings. I approached him one day as he was sitting by the unlit propane fireplace. "I am warming myself by the fire." He asked if I was alone then asked if the others were in Halifax. With one son living in Halifax, I was not sure what he was asking. I did not question who he was asking about. At this stage of his journey, he often forgot the question he was asking as soon as the answer was given. His attention span was diminishing. We conducted our usual wheelchair ride throughout the home, an activity he enjoyed when he could self-propel. He loved greeting everyone we met. We met an older nurse dressed in a pink pantsuit. As we wheeled past her, he commented, "She's looking good!"

Returning to his unit for a snack, he looked at me and said, "Are you Austin?" I stood in his full line of vision and said, "Dad, it's me, your daughter Bertha." He paused, stared at my face framed by white hair, then did a visual scan to my feet, and said "Nah!" He said he thought Bertha might come visit him today, and he laughed when I told him she might have white hair now. He stated, "They are all gone now, and all we have left are strangers, but they are all nice people . . . and they like me. The only one left is God, and he's been around a long time. I better be good!" It was not important that he no longer knew me. What was important was that he enjoyed that I pushed his wheelchair and prepared him a snack and a cup of tea with a heaping spoonful of sugar. There was a time that I was too young to know who he was, and he cared for me just the same. Life is a full circle lived with loss and cushioned by love.

One day, my sister-in-law Gloria and I took advantage of the warm weather and assisted Dad to my car for a drive, mindful that he may not understand the change in his routine. We were both surprised when he appropriately announced that we were driving on Water Street. He enjoyed seeing and commenting on the big trucks on Main Street and continued an appropriate dialogue while we bought him french fries at McDonald's. He mentioned family members he used to banter with and shared that he didn't know why he felt so mixed up on some days. We decided to drive to my brother

Walter's work site, and Dad had a big smile when he spotted his son. That day was a gift to the four of us.

Shortly thereafter, I attended mass with him as it was offered on a weekly basis in the home. Without warning, he bellowed part of the mass in Latin, indelible in his memory from years of regular attendance. Staff reported that he was often singing old French songs upon awakening and that he loved to make people jump with his sudden movements, throwing his head back with a laugh of success.

When he was cognitively alert and able to converse, his stories were always new. He told me about a man who visited him the previous evening. He called him Gerald (a name I have never heard him mention). "You know, a person should learn by the age of fifty that it is time to quit drinking and partying *avec les pattes en l'air* (with feet up in the air). The drink will eventually kill you." On that particular day, as I was preparing to leave, he said, "I live in Sluice Point. Next time you come by, I will follow you home. And next time, bring me some bubble gum."

As long as I can recall, Dad peeled and ate an apple every day until his knife was taken away from him, citing safety regulations. I decided to offer him an apple while he held on to the ribboning peeling. To my surprise, he said, "It's a Cortland." And it was. He ate most of it then said, "I'm hanging on to this second one. It's hard enough to hit someone between the eyes."

He initiated conversation less frequently yet retained positive body language. One morning, my brother wheeled him to the outdoor pond. Upon seeing the ducks, he yelled, "*Pow!*" Dad used to hunt ducks as he appreciated mom's delicious duck stew.

While his body was getting frail with a weight loss of forty-five pounds since admission and his emotions wavered, his spirit remained intact. Dad's journey continued as his vocabulary diminished. Retrieving the appropriate word often eluded him. His repeated attempts to express himself both impressed and saddened me. It was evident that he had more difficulty feeding himself. He sometimes would throw his dentures on the floor, requiring repeated trips to the denturist for repairs. Although it was difficult to watch him spill contents of his eating utensils, he wanted to be independent. Attempts to assist him resulted in a sharp look or a brisk tap on the hand. He poured his ice water in his teacup at one point, tasted the tea, then ordered me to build a fire and heat that tea on the stove. Still he could be appeased very quickly with an accepting and calm approach. Often, he extended his face for a kiss as I prepared to leave him. On one occasion, my sister-in-law Paulette, divorced from my brother years ago, accompanied me on my visit. He had not seen her in a while, and his eyes lit up at seeing her. He did not miss the opportunity to extend his face to also receive her kiss as we left.

As Dad entered his one hundred years of age, he was still teaching me about living. His limited access to words made it challenging to understand his needs. Yet despite his misspeaks, he remained patient. He would try to speak. After uttering a few words, he often smiled, shrugged his shoulders, and relaxed in acceptance of his present moment. His sleep routine became longer, sometimes extending to seventeen hours of sleep. He often woke up hungry, and despite spilling his tea and dropping food on himself, the table, and the floor, he often preferred to do it himself. He kept his independence, often wheeling himself away from visitors as his own world appeared preferable. On occasions, he would recognize visitors on sight. It was a pleasure to observe his fleeting moment of recognition. On those days, he appreciated company and would entertain with his antics and mimicking persons in his surroundings. He often would appropriately say thank you. He greeted people with a smile or a hand extended for a handshake.

My sister Marilyn posted on social media that Dad would soon be one hundred years old, encouraging people to send him a birthday card, with hopes that he would receive one hundred cards. The joy of receiving mail was reminiscent of the mail he delivered to others during his long career as a mail delivery driver. He knew all those families by name, and they knew him. He received over one thousand cards, more than he could read. However, he did enjoy many of them. Some cards and gifts were from strangers, including students and Canada Post families who shared the same occupation. For weeks, the cards arrived, attesting to the good nature of persons who wanted to make a hundred-year-old man smile.

When his hundredth birthday arrived, the family deliberated on what kind of celebration he might enjoy. We choose to invite family and friends for a midday gathering, hoping that he might be awake enough to participate and hopefully enjoy a part of it. We also invited the media. Staff had been letting Dad sleep until he awoke on his own. On that day, we made the decision to wake him early in the afternoon in order to have him participate in the celebration. He was irritable, and for a short time, I was worried. He rose to the occasion and enjoyed all the attention from family and friends, willingly posing for the media. A member of the Royal Canadian Mounted Police dropped by to extend congratulations, and on seeing the RCMP, Dad jokingly extended both his wrists as if he was going to be handcuffed. After numerous handshakes and with a crowd around him, Dad found the words for a full sentence, saying, "I have not told them I have scabies." He once again enjoyed the reaction to his humor, as we all did.

In the months that followed, it was a gift to find him alert and communicating with positive body language and the occasional appropriate word or sentence.

On Christmas Eve, I fed him one of his favorite dishes, a heaping plate of rappie pie (recipe attached), along with his protein drink and dessert. His appetite was impressive. He would occasionally pause to say "merci" and "thank you," words he often repeated, and the only words he shared with me on that visit. On Christmas Day, he was awake long enough in the afternoon to entertain visiting family with his smile and exaggerated enjoyment of Cheezies snacks. He was up in his wheelchair but slept through his turkey lunch and his hot lobster sandwich, another favorite, for his evening meal.

December 26 was a sleepy day for him. On December 27, I invited my siblings and the spouses to my home for a five o'clock meal. My brothers went in to visit Dad in the afternoon, and he slipped into his final peaceful sleep while they sat in his room. Having a planned family event allowed the family an opportunity to be gathered together to process his death. I felt as though he had chosen this time.

Life is a learning journey. What gifts and lessons did your loved one leave you?

Life is temporary. How will you live the time you have left on earth?

As for myself, I have decided to continue meeting with persons traveling through loss and grief as there is no room for pretense when one is grieving. I meet the best of the nicest people! Our public selves take a back seat as we are met with the raw emotions that make us human. That is the true experience of life, love, and loss and grief.

I have also decided to write vignettes from my own experiences that I hope you may read to lighten your journey. I have borrowed some writing prompts from a writer's workshop handout: *Old Friend from Far Away* by Nathalie Goldberg.

What I Will Miss When I Die

Every adventure that life has offered me has left me richer rather than poorer. I give credit to my parents for bringing me up in a positive home atmosphere while instilling the fear of God in me that we all die, so we better be good or else. That fear has transpired into the love of God as my knowledge expanded. A shift to spiritual awareness built into the growth and development of aging has brought me to a place of comfort and to feeling that dying isn't so bad. But still, I have my own ideas as to how I prefer it to end. Hope is a beautiful thing.

The question is, Will I miss those things that life offers if death holds a different and unimaginable bounty? My idea involves following the path my ancestors took without experiencing the hardships, of course. A visit to their time to observe how my birthplace was built. I imagine traveling throughout the creations of earth and space. I would love to be entertained by traveling within the body for a firsthand view of the changes from conception to death with an understanding of the chemicals and hormones that affect our sadness and our joy.

I think the Creator may grant these wishes of mine. Why else would he have created such intricate beauty if not for everyone to view and appreciate? Such majestic creations. Such intriguing mysteries. Why else are we all drawn to movies? They are a mere taste of the adventures death will allow. If these things are not to be, then I don't know what I shall miss. God knows I may miss nothing at all.

Attachments

Alice's Quick, Easy, and Tasty Scallop Casserole

Preheat oven to 400 degrees Fahrenheit. In an ungreased 2-quart casserole, layer 1 pound large fresh scallops, cut in two.

Cover with 1 tin (284 milliliters) of Campbell's Cream of Mushroom Soup and layer with 200 grams mozzarella cheese. Bake uncovered until cheese bubbles and forms a light crust, approximately 50 minutes.

Mom's Tomato Soup Cake

Preheat oven to 325 degrees Fahrenheit. Cream ½ cup shortening with 1 cup white sugar.

Add 1 tin Campbell's Tomato Soup (284 milliliters) in which 1 teaspoon baking soda has been dissolved.

Mix 2 cups white flour with 2 teaspoons baking powder, 1 teaspoon cinnamon, ½ teaspoon ground cloves, and 1 teaspoon nutmeg.

Add dry ingredients to wet ingredients, and fold in 1 cup raisins and 1 cup walnuts.

Place in greased and floured tube pan and bake for 50–60 minutes. Cake is done when inserted toothpick comes out clean.

Rappie Pie

Boil 1 chicken and 3 pork chops (or a pork picnic roast) with 1 celery stalk, 4 large chopped onions, and water to generate 11 cups of chicken stock.

Peel and grate 1 bucket of potatoes *or* purchase 1 small package of Acadian rapure to be used with 2 potatoes, peeled and grated.

If you are using peeled potatoes only, squeeze potato mixture in cheesecloth until only dry potato pulp remains. Discard starch liquid.

If you are using Acadian rapure mix, add 2 grated potatoes with starch liquid to mix.

Remove meat from stock and shred in bite-size pieces. Pour stock over potato (rapure) mixture while mixing continuously. The faster you add the broth, the better. Add ½ handful salt and pepper to taste.

Prepare one 9 × 12 foil pan by greasing with bacon fat.

Pour ½ potato mixture in prepared pan. Layer with shredded meat. Cover with remaining rapure.

Bake in preheated 400-degree-Fahrenheit oven for 30 minutes. Lower heat to 300 degrees Fahrenheit. Bake an additional 3 hours. Butter or pork scraps on top of dish will create a better crust.

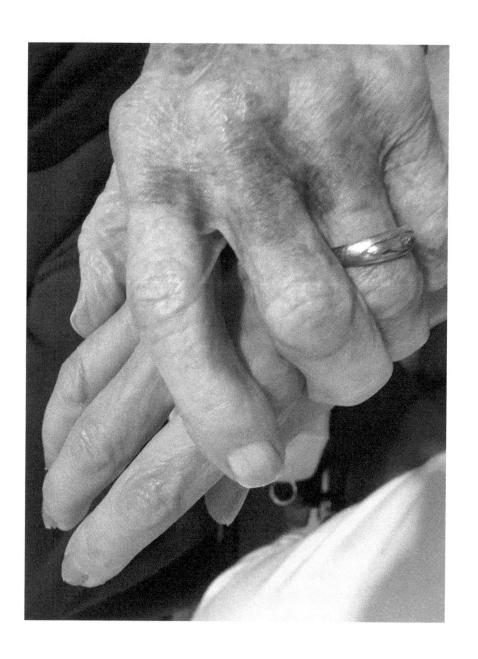

REFERENCES

Worden, J. William. 1982. *Grief Counseling and Grief Therapy*. Springer Publishing Company.

James, John W., and Russel Friedman. 2009. *The Grief Recovery Handbook*. Collins Living: HarperCollins Publishers.

Smith, Douglas. 1999. *Being a Wounded Healer*. Psycho-Spiritual Publications.

Bryson, Ken A., ed. 1987. *Reflections on Dying and Death*. Sentinel Printing Limited.

Marchiano, Bruce. 2004. *Jesus Wept*. Howard Publishing.

CPSIA information can be obtained
at www.ICGtesting.com
Printed in the USA
BVHW031116090519
547846BV00004B/54/P

9 781796 031669